# DEMYSTIFYING ACTION RESEARCH MANUAL FOR BASIC EDUCATION TEACHERS

## *From Proposal to Presentation*

***Prof. Resty C. Samosa LPT, PhD-SciEd.***

***Prof. Rodrigo Mison Dantay, Jr. LPT, PhD-DEM, DPA, DLitt.***

ISBN:
Hardbound- 978-621-470-396-8
MOBI/KINDLE-978-621-470-397-5
Softbound/Paperback-978-621-470-398-2

Published by:
Poetry Planet Book Publishing House
Rosario, Pozorrubio, Pangasinan, Philippines
Contact Number: 09554960094

# PREFACE

This research manual was developed to guide beginning action researchers in the onset and outset of their research exploration experiences. It will serve as their guiding light in the process of starting, pursuing and completing the action research report.

This research manual contains brief overview of action research based on the Department of Education memorandum that provides information on the very nature of research.

To set mood and heighten motivation, this research manual includes purposes, significance, advantages, gains, benefits, opportunities and positive impact and implications take from studies to ease researcher's burden in pursuing this kind of undertaking.

Most importantly, it provides techniques and tips in processing data, in the simplest, easiest, most practical, convenient, and researcher- friendly way without compromising standards. All these directly came from experiences, trainings and practices of action research practitioners, who find such undertaking truly a beneficial, effective, and contributory endeavor to the profession and the improvement of education in general and the teaching – learning process, in particular.

Options for models and formats in various settings are included in this research manual while illustrative example of output and reports are readily available for adoption, pattern or guide for researchers.

The segments on frequently – asked- questions guide beginners. It would also help out researchers in concretizing their concepts on action research and in coming up with their own work.

Furthermore, there are bucket list of terms as reference for the choice of words in the title, the in-text citation, data analysis, presentation of conclusion and the use of the concepts transitional markers. Some templates are displayed for utilization that can also be modified and/or enhanced, if necessary.

With all these features this research manual would be a great help to action researchers in their desire to pursue classroom action research which hopefully will bring great effect, positive turn- out and high impact outcome to the community and humanity.

# TABLE OF CONTENTS

# CHAPTER 1

## ACTION RESEARCH: ITS MEANING AND PERSPECTIVES

**Learning Competencies**

*At the end of this module, teachers should be able to:*

1. Define action research in the context of teaching practice;
2. Explain each of the three principles of action research framework—excellence, integrity, and openness;
3. Describe each stage of the action research framework and explain how each one is related to one another;
4. Enumerate the steps in operationalizing the action research framework; and
5. Apply conceptually the five stages of the action research framework on a specific problem situation in the classroom.
6. Understand the importance of action research in education.
7. Enumerate the limitation of action research
8. Discuss the characteristics of action research as a methodology for teachers
9. Identify the types of action research.

### Action Research in the Context of Teaching Practice

Teachers are essential part of the educational system, they are entrusted by the public and private institutions to impart knowledge, assist the learners to develop skills, and correct attitude toward self, developing learners holistically leading to development of life-long learners. In order to achieve these goals, teachers must be able to possess 21st century skills and be able to address problems inside the classroom.

Many reasons have been suggested for the lack of classroom change: the transmission view of teaching that teachers have is rarely critiqued in teacher education programmes, courses are too theoretical and neglect the practical needs; teachers distrust academic research as it fails to account for the differences between schools; and a lack of follow up support as teachers try to develop their pedagogical practice. Because of these difficulties, there is a growing emphasis on using action research for teacher professional development.

In a nut shell, action research is a systematic inquiry into practice, with the intention of understanding and improving it. Action Research as "a form of self-reflective inquiry undertaken by participants in social (including educational) situations in order to improve the rationality and justice of (a) their own social or educational practices; (b) their understanding of these practices; and, (c) the situations in which these practices are carried out". In this definition Action Research goes beyond technical solutions, and tries to obtain a commitment towards improving practices, basing the said on a critical understanding of the practice and on the situation in which the practice takes place.

Action Research, by definition of the Department of Education, is a process of systematic and reflective inquiry to improve educational practices or resolve problems in the classroom or the school. It is a process of uncovering solutions to classroom or school problems through a series of methodical, logical, and organized activities. The outcome of these activities is the enhancement of classroom and school practices.

Action Research design follows a cyclical process. First, the researcher identifies a problem and determines a plan of action to address it. Then, the action plan is implemented, and data is gathered to determine the effects of the action implemented. The information gathered during the implementation phase is analyzed and evaluated to gain a better understanding of the problem and determine the effectiveness of solution implemented. Action research is pragmatic and solution - driven, and any information gathered is used to identify and implement a solution to the problem (Samosa, 2020).

Action research is a design that involves a process which is iterative involving preliminary identification of current issues encountered by a teacher, in collaboration with other stakeholders, which lead to planning a plausible teaching strategy to address the pressing issue, evaluation of the impact of the designed instructional activities, and reflecting on the outcomes of these activities (Aguja, and Prudente, 2017).

Action Research can be used to make small improvements in individual practices and/or influence institutional change. However, institutional change seldom occurs from improvement in an individual's practice. Thus, in most of its forms, Action Research is a collaborative activity involving others as co-researchers. The co-researchers study the situation, plan actions, implement them and engage in self and collective reflection. Action Research requires ongoing validation from an educated audience able to judge the authenticity and relevance of the research in a professional context. Initially it involves the researcher giving a true account of her/his practice and justifying it through drawing on professional knowledge available through others' research. As it progresses, it moves on to testing the research with colleagues both within and outside the research context, and finally goes public to convince others of the validity of the claims.

Within education, the main goal of action research is to determine ways to enhance the lives of learners. At the same time, action research can enhance the lives of those professionals who work within educational systems. To illustrate, action research has been directly linked to the professional growth and development of teachers.

Action research (a) helps teachers develop new knowledge directly related to their classrooms, (b) promotes reflective teaching and thinking, (c) expands teachers' pedagogical repertoire, (d) puts teachers in charge of their craft, (e) reinforces the link between practice and student achievement, (f) fosters an openness toward new ideas and learning new things, and (g) gives teachers ownership of effective practices. Moreover, action research workshops can be used to replace traditional, ineffective teacher in-service training as a means for professional development activities. To be effective, teacher in-service training needs to be extended over multiple sessions, contain active learning to allow teachers to manipulate the ideas and enhance their assimilation of the information, and align the concepts presented with the current curriculum, goals, or teaching concerns.

Therefore, providing teachers with the necessary skills, knowledge, and focus to engage in meaningful inquiry about their professional practice will enhance this practice, and effect positive changes concerning the educative goals of the learning community.

From this, the state policy to establish, maintain, and support a complete, adequate, and integrated system of education pertinent to the needs of the people, the country, and the society-at-large is the foundation for the creation of Republic Act 10533 titled "An Act Enhancing the Philippine Basic Education System by Strengthening its Curriculum and Increasing the Number of Years for Basic Education," otherwise known as the "Enhanced Basic Education Act of 2013." One of the mandates of the Enhanced Basic Education Act of 2013 is the delivery of a curriculum that is relevant, responsive, and research-based. In line with this, the role of research in education is strengthened and integrated in both curriculum and instruction.

Research is envisioned to serve as concrete guide in steering both policy and practice in the educational system. To ensure relevance, responsiveness, and usefulness of studies in the production of fact-based policy and practice in the Department of Education (DepEd), the following Action Research process is designed. It serves as the first step in achieving the national goal of inculcating and propagating a culture of research from the grassroots of Philippine education to the highest levels of public-school governance. This strategic step is a vehicle toward the direction of realizing the legal mandate on conducting research as part of the DepEd's institutional target for each governance level in fulfilment of the Department's mission, vision and core values.

## Guiding Principles

Implementation of Action Research includes Guiding Principles that support continuity, progression, and participation in all governance levels. These principles show the path for research facilitators and researchers (include school heads, teachers, administrators, and instruction-related and non-teaching personnel) in the delivery of research-based instruction and its necessary support anchored to DepEd's vision (figure 1.1), mission (figure 1.2), core values (figure 1.3), and strategic directions (figure 1.4).

**The DepEd Vision**

We dream of Filipinos who passionately love their country and whose values and competencies enable them to realize their full potential and contribute meaningfully to building the nation. As a learner-centered public institution, the Department of Education continuously improves itself to better serve its stakeholders

**Figure 1.1. DepEd's Vision**

**The DepEd Mission**

To protect and promote the right of every Filipino to quality, equitable, culture-based, and complete basic education
where:
**Students** learn in a child-friendly, gender-sensitive, safe, and motivating environment.
**Teachers** facilitate learning and constantly nurture every learner.
**Administrators and staff**, as stewards of the institution, ensure an enabling and supportive environment for effective learning to happen.
**Family, community, and other stakeholders** are actively engaged and share responsibility for developing life-long learners.

**Figure 1.2. DepEd's Mission**

**Our Core Values**
Maka-Diyos
Maka-tao
Makakalikasan
Makabansa

**Figure 1.3. DepEd's Core Values**

**Strategic Directions**
By 2022, DepEd is a modern, professional, proactive, nimble, trusted, and nurturing institution delivering quality, accessible, relevant, and liberating K to 12 Education, enabling our learners to be nation-loving, resilient, and complete lifelong learners.

**Figure 1.4. DepEd's Strategic Directions**

The provisions of DepEd Order No. 39, s. 2016 (Adoption of the Basic Education Research Agenda) have paved the way for the advancement of a concrete research agenda in Philippine basic education system that include the themes teaching and learning, child protection, human resource development, and governance. These themes serve as basis for the generation of topics that can be explored for the purpose of formulating research-based and sound policies.

DepEd's vision, mission, core values, and strategic directions serve as the foundation in the conduct of educational research among practitioners. Action Research strengthens educational policies by encouraging continuous improvement of services to its primary clients, the learners, thereby contributing to the achievement of educational goals. It is essentially a professionally meaningful scientific endeavor that is significant, proactive, manageable, and empowering. Teachers who engage in Action Research have the distinct privilege and rare opportunity of ensuring a school environment that is both supportive and enabling of learners. In order to accomplish these, the following guiding principles in the conduct of Action Research are suggested

**Principle 1: Excellence**

If Action Research is intended to influence educational decisions and actions, it must, first and foremost, adhere to the highest level of quality. The principle of excellence demands that the topic of inquiry be relevant and researchable, the methods applied be appropriate, and the findings be logical, coherent, and supported by data. Research designs will vary depending on the objectives of the study, but regardless of which design is used, researchers must apply rigorous empirical methods on which scientific inquiry is grounded.

**Principle 2: Integrity**

The highest ethical standards must be employed by Action Researchers, most especially when the study involves the participation of people. Researchers must ensure that the study will not cause harm on human respondents. Informed consent must be obtained from research participants, ensuring that they are cognizant of the general purpose of the study and that all efforts are expended to prevent them from being exposed to unusual risk. Consistent with the principle of excellence, the principle of integrity also requires honesty and accuracy in the collection and analysis of data and the reporting of results.

**Principle 3: Openness**

One of the keys to successful conduct of Action Research is collaboration. In line with this, the idea of openness gives emphasis to the need to engage more partners in Action Research that bring multidisciplinary perspectives to any inquiry, considering that research agenda in basic education is quite extensive.

Dissemination of research results must be accurate and opportune. It should be arranged within the limits of confidentiality, safeguarding anonymity of participants and sanctity of the findings, and shared with stakeholders for appreciation, application, and evaluation.

To ensure the application of these principles, the following five protocols should be observed in the conduct of Action Research within the context of DepEd.

**Protocol 1: Reducing the risk of harm**

Action Research should not bring harm to participants. If a study needs to be done despite the possibility that participants could be put in danger or in a situation that makes them feel some discomfort, there must be strong justification for pursuing it prior to the collection of data. Contingency plans for reducing harm or discomfort and/or detailed debriefing procedures should be spelled out in a written informed consent to be signed by each participant/respondentof their own free will. Types of harm that they can be subjected to include physical harm, psychological distress and discomfort, psychosocial disadvantage, financial problems, and invasion of privacy and anonymity.

**Protocol 2: Securing informed consent**

One of the procedures followed in keeping with research ethics is the securing of informed consent. It is a document that informs participants what their involvement in the study entails and what sensitive information might have to be asked from them. It also includes the purpose of the research, the methods to be used, and the possible outcomes as well as the demands, discomforts, inconveniences, and risks that the participants may experience

**Protocol 3: Safeguarding confidentiality and anonymity**

Safeguarding the anonymity of research participants and the confidentiality of the information they provide is another important component in Action Research. At no point should their identities and other personal information about them be divulged to other individuals without their permission. Documents that bear their names, identities, and other sensitive information must be placed in a secure place that is accessible only to the researcher/s. The same documents may be disposed of through shredding after one year of research dissemination. Mere dumping of such documents in trash bins or "recyclable" receptacles is improper.

**Protocol 4: Avoiding deceptive practices.**

Action Researchers should avoid deceptive practices. It is their obligation to make the research participants understand the objectives of the study and the specific tasks that they (participants) have to do to provide the data needed. Although deception is sometimes necessary in order to obtain valid results, particularly when delicate information is to be obtained, participants should eventually be debriefed of the true objectives of the study.

**Protocol 5: Ensuring justice and fidelity**

Fairness is another ethical practice that should be followed in conducting Action Research. This is an important consideration particularly in situations where the rights of an individual or group may affect those of another. To be just, implies that the researcher adheres to the standards of impartiality, equality, and reciprocity in relating with research participants. Fidelity refers to being loyal and truthful to the respondents by keeping promises to them such as the anonymity of the respondents' identities and respecting their dignity as persons. Researchers should keep these things in mind as they interact with individuals who participate in their studies.

**Action Research mechanism**

Action Research becomes a means for informed decisions in the field of education.

The following are some examples.

1. **Continuous improvement of research agenda and standards.**

   DepEd has adopted the Basic Education Research Agenda (BERA) with the issuance of DepEd Order No. 39, s. 2016. BERA provides a road map for DepEd and its stakeholders in the conduct of research and in the utilization of research results for planning, policy formulation, and program development in alignment with its vision, mission, and core values. The research agenda is expected to build on findings from existing research, generate new knowledge on priority areas of study, focus on relevant education issues, and maximize the use of available resources for research within and outside the department. The principles of excellence, integrity, and openness are the backbones of the BERA. Each theme under the BERA has a unique contribution to the attainment of the department's official mandate and projected outcomes. Teaching and learning respond to students' and teachers' needs and address the quality of education. Child protection focuses on students' safety and security and directly enhances access to education. Human resource development pertains to concerns on teaching and nonteaching staff, while governance examines administration and stakeholder engagement. In addition to the four major themes specified in the BERA, DepEd also recognizes three current areas of inquiry that cut across the themes: (1) disaster risk reduction and management (DRRM), (2) gender and development, and (3) inclusive education. Essentially, the research agenda presents trends and issues that can spur new insights about classroom practices and practical solutions to classroom problems upon investigation. More importantly, the research agenda can orient and advise policy makers on matters that necessitate the formulation of policy statements. Periodic review of the BERA vis-à-vis consolidated research results, new education trends, and emerging education issues will enable the department to adjust strategies in promoting the conduct of Action Research.

2. **Action Research training through LAC session**

   Continuing professional development of teachers anchored on the principle of lifelong learning and DepEd's commitment to the enrichment of teachers' potentials are expressed in the issuance of DepEd Order No. 35, s. 2016, which institutes Learning Action Cell (LAC) as school-based continuing professional development strategy in the K-12 basic education program for the purpose of improving teaching and learning. The LAC's primary function is the creation of a professional learning community among teachers with the same school to help them improve their practice and enhance learners' achievement. Through LAC sessions, the vision of developing a "culture of research" is expected to gradually materialize by providing teachers the necessary training and technical assistance in conducting Action Research. DepEd's outcomes-based policy should guide schools in the implementation of the Action Research as a means of promoting scientific inquiry for the purpose of improving instruction and learning outcomes. The school-based Action Research training will provide teachers with basic knowledge and skills for initiating learner-focused interventions that address learning gaps and issues within their classrooms in order to upgrade learning outcomes. School-based LAC sessions are planned and scheduled by the school head with the assistance of the school LAC facilitator. LAC plan for each school shall include the full Action Research training when deemed necessary or selected Action Research topics according to the training needs of teachers. Facilitator's Guides for Action Research training help school facilitators lead LAC sessions on the essentials of Action Research. Action Research Guides correspond to topics serve as basic resource materials for teachers and as supplementary materials to the LAC sessions. The Action Research framework, Action Research designs, data collection and analysis methods, and Action Research writing are all covered in the training through a series of LAC sessions. The use of LAC meetings as training sessions for Action Research is a step toward fulfilling the DepEd's commitment to help equip teachers in engaging in Action Research. It is a way of enhancing teachers' potentials for self and professional development. Technical assistance will be provided through a continuous system of consultation, mentoring, and coaching of training participants in the course of the LAC sessions.

3. **Analysis of results for policy recommendation**

After completion of the Action Research training through LAC sessions, teachers are expected to work individually or collaboratively on an Action Research project. Results of Action Research undertaken by teachers will be compiled and synthesized for discussion on how they can be utilized for policy recommendations. DepEd Order No. 13, s. 2015, which establishes a Policy Development Process at the DepEd, provides systematic, evidence-based, and participatory mechanisms and procedures for the formulation, adoption, and review of policies. Policies recommended based on findings of Action Research projects should be anchored on DepEd's vision, mission, and core values to ensure that these are geared towards effective and efficient attainment of education outcomes. Discussions on the results of Action Research may be conducted during LAC sessions so that policy recommendations can come from teachers themselves. The school head may organize a LAC session solely for the discussion of results of Action Research projects in the school. The formulation of policy for recommendation shall then be agreed through the participation of relevant stakeholders. Sound Action Research findings, recommendations from experts, and insights from relevant stakeholders all contribute to the process of articulating evidence-based policy recommendations. Proposed policies may be submitted to the DepEd Central Office through the Planning Service-Policy Research and Development Division (PS-PRD) for management-level discussion and, possibly, endorsement for approval.

4. **Dissemination and adoption of policy through evidence-based research.**

DepEd Order No. 13, s. 2015, which promotes evidenced-based policy formulation, supports one of the provisions of the Basic Education Act of 2001 (Republic Act 9155). The provision mandates the "undertaking of educational research and studies that will serve as one of the bases for necessary reforms and policy development" (RA 9155 Chapter 1, Sec. 5–7). Once a policy recommendation is approved, it shall then be disseminated for adoption through an issuance of guidelines in the form of an order from the DepEd Central Office. A school, division, or regional office can disseminate the research results with their policy recommendations among their teachers in the form of research conferences, research forums, and policy forums. Research proponents and research managers can share their research findings, gather new inputs and research ideas, and discuss policy options based on research results. Publication in research journals, research bulletins, and studies archival mechanisms for completed studies are options for wider dissemination. Utilization of research results by teachers through incorporation of proven effective interventions in their classroom instruction and adoption of the policy recommendations of research will improve learning outcomes and governance processes.

## Action Research Process and Framework

The Action Research framework serves as the structural basis for procedures from the first step of identifying a topic to the last step of analyzing research data and reflecting upon the results, which, in turn, can be the beginning of another study following a cyclical series of activities. The framework guides Action Researchers in working through the process of finding a focus and design for the study, collecting and analyzing data, and drawing conclusions (figure 1). It involves five (5) stages known as the 5 A's: Assess the situation, **A**sk a question, **A**ct to seeks answers, **A**cquire information, and **A**nalyze and reflect on the results.

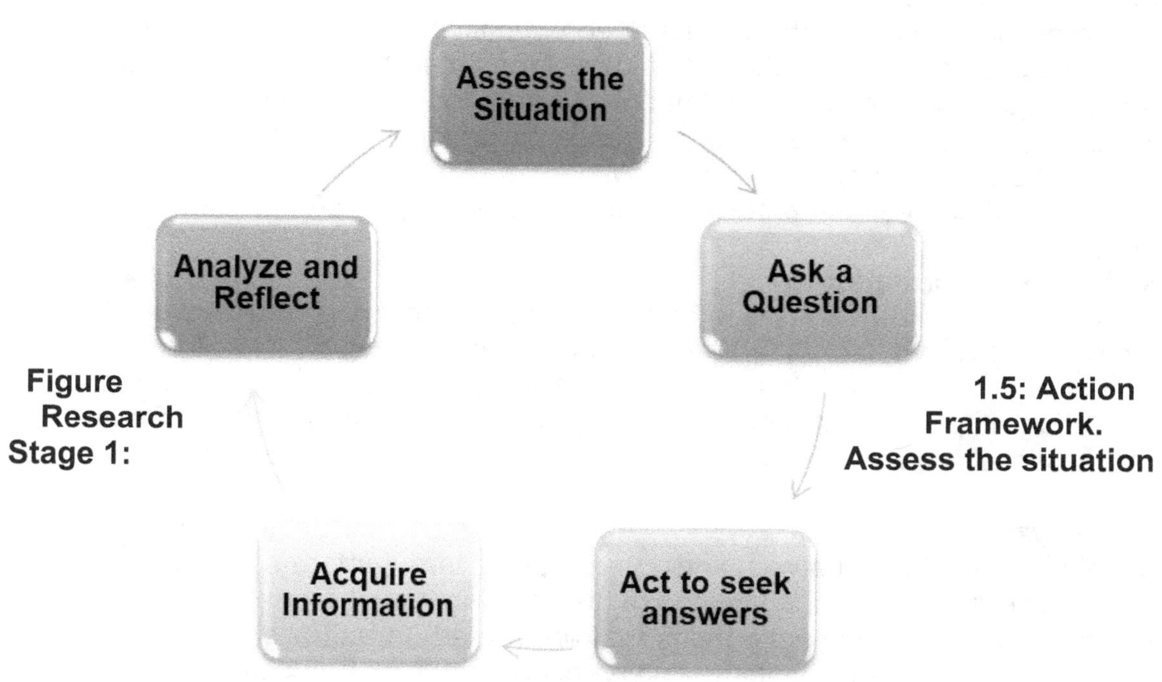


**Figure 1.5: Action Research Framework. Stage 1: Assess the situation**

At this initial stage, practitioners identify improvement opportunities in the teaching and learning process. Also called reconnaissance in other Action Research models, this stage involves examination of school environment, academic programs, instructional practices, and learners. Specifically, it is during this stage that teachers ruminate on student outcomes (achievements and dispositions), curriculum (standards, competencies, and instructional materials), instruction (teaching strategies, use of technology), school climate (student and teacher morale, relationships between students and teachers and between teachers and supervisors), and parental involvement (attendance at events, involvement in parent-teacher committees).

**Stage 2: Ask a question**

The research question is a clear, focused, concise, complex, and arguable question where the research is centered in. It is central to an Action Research project as it gives focus to it and guides all stages of inquiry, from the determination of the methods for data collection and analysis and to the writing of the research report. Action Research is different from other types of research in that the researcher has to go beneath the surface of a classroom problem or instructional/learning issue in order to identify a topic. A practitioner also needs to ask why something is happening or not in order to generate a research question. During this stage, the teacher tries to gain insight into the problem by looking for its root cause and thinking of a possible solution.

**Stage 3: Act to seek answers**

When an Action Research topic has been identified based on an observed problem or issue, a tentative solution should be formulated from a careful review of literature. It is then methodically implemented, either for one single learner or for an entire class. To be able to answer the research question, the teacher has to design and test an appropriate intervention with a view of ultimately solving it. The intervention should address the problem or issue or at least part of it.

**Stage 4: Acquire information.**

This stage entails gathering information (data) about the intervention as implemented. Certain types of information require specific ways of collection. The researcher should choose the data collection instructions that are appropriate for the intervention implemented and for the Action Research question. Some research questions require quantitative data while others necessitate qualitative data.

**Stage 5: Analyze and reflect.**

In this stage, data analysis and interpretation are performed. When an Action Researcher reflects on the findings of his or her inquiry, he or she is able to derive conclusions and recommendations that are rooted on and aligned with the results. He or she can decide if the intervention that has been implemented responds to the problem or issue earlier identified.

**Operationalizing the Action Research Framework**

The Action Research framework is a philosophical and theoretical structure that defines the key points in Action Research in five (5) stages. These stages are concretized or operationalized in five major steps or activities that take after the scientific method, which essentially determine the reasonableness or acceptability of a hypothesis about the effectiveness of a proposed intervention as an attempt to solve a classroom problem or issue. The following are the steps in operationalizing the Action Research framework in one's own investigation.

1. **Identifying the Action Research problem.**

   The most critical step in research is knowing what the problem is. Defining the classroom problem or issue that needs to be solved helps a researcher decide on what specific intervention is suitable. Once an intervention has been devised, the researcher can plan on what information has to be collected and how.

2. **Designing the Action Research.**

   A research design is simply a set of related procedures that have to be followed in order to generate relevant information with minimal effort, time, and money. Experimental and qualitative research designs are two methods that can be applied when testing the effectiveness of an intervention depending on its nature and the extent to which the researcher can control variables. Action Researchers can either choose to collect numerical data, in which case an experimental design is appropriate. He or she may also choose to collect descriptive data, which requires a qualitative design. Prior to the enforcement of an intervention, Action Researchers can conduct a preliminary assessment of the problem situation (stage 1 of the Action Research framework) using any of the other major research designs, namely, causal comparative (or ex-post facto), correlational, and survey.

3. **Collecting data for Action Research.**

   Data collected after intervention has been implemented gives a clear picture of the effect of the teacher's action on the variables of interest. Post-intervention data may be obtained through paper-and-pencil instruments, interviews, observations, or documents and materials. While one data collection method is sufficient, a combination of quantitative and qualitative data collection methods (called mixed methods) is often preferred and profitable for the research.

4. **Analyzing data for Action Research.**

   Data analysis may be performed using the appropriate statistical technique for numerical data or qualitative analysis for descriptive (narrative) data. Descriptive and inferential statistics are useful for data collected using tests and rating scales. Examination of recurring themes or patterns (qualitative analysis) is most appropriate for data obtained from interviews, observations, or documents and materials.

5. **Writing the Action Research report.**

   The Action Research report contains a detailed description of the problem situation or issue, the intervention applied, the methods used in collecting and analyzing data, and the findings of the study. Several types of reports (from executive summary to conference paper) may be produced, but it is important to complete the full research report first before coming up with synthesized versions.

The results of the research must be reported not only to the participants and other stakeholders, but also to those who need the information in making critical decisions. This help ensures that the decisions they come up with are grounded on sound and objective research findings and are not just subjectively formulated based on personal preferences and inclinations.

## Action Research Implementation Model

All of the key concepts in the Action Research framework and the corresponding steps for its operationalization comprise the Action Research Implementation Model (see figure 1.6). Direction and guidance for Action Research are provided by the principles of the DepEd as expressed in its vision, mission, and core values as well as the research strategic directions formulated for the department. The method by which Action Research is implemented is called the Action Research Mechanism. This involves three practices, namely: (1) continuous improvement of the research agenda and standards, (2) Action Research training conducted through Learning Action Cell (LAC) sessions, and (3) analysis of research results for policy recommendations.

Teachers engage in classroom-based investigation following the Action Research framework, a philosophical, theoretical structure composed of five stages (Assess the situation, Ask a question, Act to seek answers, Acquire information, and Analyze and reflect).

It is operationalized through the five (5) steps or activities of the Action Research process (identifying the research problem, designing the action research, collecting data, analyzing data, and writing the action research report). All the five activities, particularly the last one, are considered for Policy Recommendation, Adoption, and Dissemination. Finally, through Monitoring and Evaluation and Provision of Technical Assistance, policy recommendations are examined so that adjustments in the DepEd vision, mission, core values, and research strategic directions can be appropriately initiated.

## Feedback Mechanism

The following are the different feedback mechanisms utilized in the conduct of Action Research.

1. **Monitoring and evaluation.** The Schools Division Research Committee is responsible for ensuring that Action Research projects are reliably monitored by those who supervise the teacher/s conducting it. They should also

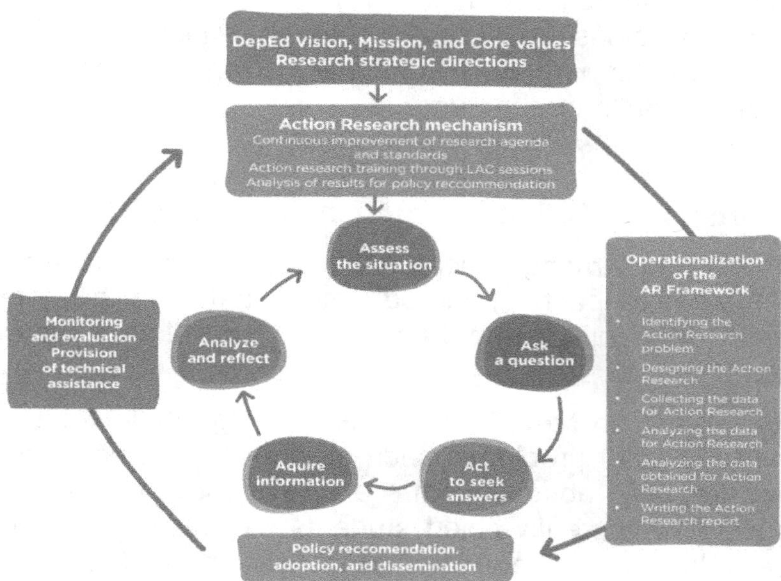


**Figure 1.6.** Action Research implementation model

ensure and verify that the conduct of research conforms to the Action Research proposal and work plan as approved. To track the progress of approved proposals, research managers have to conduct random visits or inspection at research sites and discuss with the researchers the status of their studies.

They may ask for progress reports from researchers and interview them regarding their investigations. Other feedback mechanisms may be worked out between research managers and researchers according to their situations and needs. E-mails may be used as means of obtaining updates on ongoing research projects. For continuous improvement of the management of Action Research, research managers in the national, regional, and division levels have to conduct regular and prescheduled monitoring of approved Action Research proposals and initiatives. Information solicited through monitoring activities should lead to the improvement of the feedback mechanism.

2. **Provision of technical assistance**. Research managers are expected to provide technical assistance to researchers when the need for such is expressed through feedback and monitoring schemes. They are to assist researchers in formulating Action Research questions, developing and implementing pertinent and relevant interventions, collecting and analyzing data, and writing the research report. They should also support researchers who use LAC sessions as means of disseminating results. In other words, their role will be that of mentor and coach for teacher investigators. Whenever necessary, research managers may also conduct or supervise the conduct of LAC sessions on Action Research, wherein Facilitators' Guides, Teacher's Guides, related documents, and other relevant resources are made available for their use.

**Understanding the Importance of Action research in Education.**

Action Research is popular among educators because there is always room for improvement when it comes to teaching and educating students. The following are some of the reasons why Action Research is valuable to stakeholders in the educational system.

1. **Results of Action Research benefit students**. Through Action Research, effective solutions to student problems, such as poor school performance, low motivation, or frequent absenteeism, can be identified and applied. Research on special or differently-abled students can also help teachers practice inclusive education in a way that will be profitable to them. Successful interventions for various types of learning difficulties can provide teachers with options that can be utilized in practicing differentiated instruction

2. **Action Research promotes the culture of research among teachers**. It is imperative for teachers to resolve problems in their own classrooms and schools. Teachers who engage in scientific inquiry in addressing classroom 22or school issues and problems are those who are keen on improving the educational practice, which, eventually, will contribute to the promotion of accessibility and quality of education, as well as its governance (DepEd Order No. 43, s. 2015). Among the areas that teachers can explore in Action Research are solutions for problems about least learned skills and competencies. At the very least, Action Research can help teachers understand what is happening in their classroom and identify changes that need to be put in place for the advancement of both teaching and learning experience. Finally, and more importantly, Action Research can help

answer the questions that teachers have about instructional strategies, student performance, and classroom management techniques.

3. **Action Research serves as one of the bases for necessary reforms and policy development (DepEd Order No. 16, s. 2017).** Results of classroom research are important sources of inputs for decision- and policy-makers in modifying or replacing current directives and regulations, as well as commonly accepted practices, particularly those that are no longer effective or relevant to learners in the present contexts. Problems or issues encountered by teachers in the classroom are like red flags that point to instructional limitations and deficiencies. When several Action Research conducted by different teacher-investigators come to the same conclusions, they can lead to valuable action on the part of educational leaders and administrators. Even if conclusions from studies undertaken by different researchers on the same topic seem to contradict each other, these still offer important information that can be the starting point for revisions of old policies and practices or creation of new ones.

### Difference Between Action Research and Fundamental Research

The table below summarizes the difference between the action research and fundamental research (Bermudo, 2020)

| Element of Research | Action Research | Fundamental Research |
|---|---|---|
| **Ultimate Goal** | Improve the professional practice (problem in professional practice) | Contribute to the knowledge in the field (identify the problem based on the literature) |
| **Type of problem** | Practical problem (directly or indirectly experienced by the researcher) | Research problem (based on the gap identified in the literature) |
| **Investigator** | Teachers and schools' administrators (practitioner) | Individual who are remote from the environment they are studying). |
| **Level of involvement** | Participants could be actively involved from the start to the end of the study. | Participant are normally involved during the data collection stage only. |

The primary attribute that separate action research from other types research is its focus on practical issues in the classroom as well as having those involved from the start to finish of the research undertaking unlike fundamental research were participants are only involved during data gathering as the source of data. Action research focuses on issues that are specific and personal to teachers in their own classrooms and schools, with the primarily goal of improving professional practice. People learn best and more willing to apply what they have learned when examining an issue or problem themselves. The research takes place in real – world situations and aims to solve real problems. The researcher studies the problem systematically and ensures any change that is made is informed by the evidence he or she has collected, and then shares the results of that research.

## Characteristics of Action Research as a Methodology for teachers

1. Action research rejects positivist notions of rationality, objectivity, and truth and instead has an openness to competing possibilities for effective pedagogical practice in educational contexts;
2. Action research employs educators' reflective and interpretive categories, and uses the language of educators as a basis for educators to explore and develop their own pedagogical theorizing;
3. Action research allows educators' unrealized self-understandings to be discerned by analyzing their own practices and understandings;
4. Action research connects reflection to action, enabling educators to overcome barriers to pedagogical change through awareness of social and systemic factors influencing their educational context;
5. Action research involves deep consideration of theory and practice and to demonstrate this critically self-reflective action, researchers develop and organize knowledge in which truth is evidenced through its relation to practice.

## Limitation of Action research

As discussed in the earlier part, research promotes the best intervention in solving real life problems. However, just like any type of research, it has also limitation such as:

1. **Relatively unknown.** Action research is unknown compared to the fundamental research way of conducting research. The majority are familiar with the fundamental research because many books are written about it. Very few write an action research and there are also differences on how people conduct action research because most of training focuses on fundamental approaches in research. In graduate studies also, the focus of research subject is on fundamental approaches.
2. **Difficult to conduct**. Time constraint hinders teachers to engage in action research. Ideally an action research takes approximately six months

depending on the purpose of the study. With the complexities of teacher's role and functions, engaging in action research entails a lot of motivation and courage among them. In terms of competence and confidence to try action research, teachers are confused about how to incorporate action research in their attempt to improve their own practice. This can be attributed to its nature which requires the competence of the teacher-researcher to implement.

3. **Validity of research**. Action research is prone to bias. It does not conform with many of the requirement of the fundamental research with which one may be familiar. Fundamental research has well – defined steps and utilize a more complex way of gathering and analyzing data that are not incorporated in the action research process. Sometimes the output of action research is doubted by some because of its lenient process.
4. **Results are not generalizable**. Action research question relates only to a specific situation. Each class is unique with a unique combination of characteristics. Therefore, each class has unique problem that is solved in a unique way also. What is effective in class. A may not be effective in Class B. The result is so narrow that generalizing it to a wider context is not feasible.
5. **Difficult to write up results**. Since it is less structured compared to fundamental research, writing and presenting the results of action research is difficult. Drawing meaningful information out of the data collected needs expertise from the researcher most specially if qualitative approach is employed.

## Types of Action Research

Part of the confusion we find when we hear the term "action research" is that there are different types of action research depending upon the participants involved. A plan of research can involve a single teacher investigating an issue in his or her classroom, a group of teachers working on a common problem, or a team of teachers and others focusing on a school- or district-wide issue.

1. **Individual teacher research** usually focuses on a single issue in the classroom. The teacher may be seeking solutions to problems of classroom management, instructional strategies, use of materials, or student learning. Teachers may have support of their supervisor or principal, an instructor for a course they are taking, or parents. The problem is one that the teacher believes is evident in his or her classroom and one that can be addressed on an individual basis. The research may then be such that the teacher collects data or may involve looking at student participation. One of the drawbacks of individual research is that it may not be shared with others unless the teacher chooses to present findings at a faculty meeting, make a formal presentation at a conference, or submit written material to a listserv,

journal, or newsletter. It is possible for several teachers to be working concurrently on the same problem with no knowledge of the work of others.

2. **Collaborative action research** may include as few as two teachers or a group of several teachers and others interested in addressing a classroom or department issue. This issue may involve one classroom or a common problem shared by many classrooms. These teachers may be supported by individuals outside of the school, such as a university or community partner.
3. **School-wide research** focuses on issues common to all. For example, a school may have a concern about the lack of parental involvement in activities, and is looking for a way to reach more parents to involve them in meaningful ways. Or, the school may be looking to address its organizational and decision-making structures. Teams of staff from the school work together to narrow the question, gather and analyze the data, and decide on a plan of action. An example of action research for a school could be to examine their state test scores to identify areas that need improvement, and then determine a plan of action to improve student performance. Team work and individual contributions to the whole are very important, and it may be that problem points arise as the team strives to develop a process and make commitments to each other. When these obstacles are overcome, there will be a sense of ownership and accomplishment in the results that come from this school-wide effort.
4. **District-wide research** is far more complex and utilizes more resources, but the rewards can be great. Issues can be organizational, community-based, performance-based, or processes for decision-making. A district may choose to address a problem common to several schools or one of organizational management. Downsides are the documentation requirements (communication) to keep everyone in the loop, and the ability to keep the process in motion. Collecting data from all participants needs a commitment from staff to do their fair share and to meet agreed-upon deadlines for assignments. On the positive side, real school reform and change can take hold based on a common understanding through inquiry. The involvement of multiple constituent groups can lend energy to the process and create an environment of genuine stakeholders.

**Types of action research**

| | Individual teacher research | Collaborative action research | School-wide action research | District-wide action research |
|---|---|---|---|---|
| **Focus** | Single classroom issue | Single classroom or several classrooms with common issue | School issue, problem, or area of collective interest | District issue Organizational structures |
| **Possible support needed** | Coach/mentor Access to technology Assistance with data organization and analysis | Substitute teachers Release time Close link with administrators | School commitment Leadership Communication External partners | District commitment Facilitator Recorder Communication External partners |
| **Potential impact** | Curriculum Instruction Assessment | Curriculum Instruction Assessment Policy | Potential to impact school restructuring and change Policy Parent involvement Evaluation of programs | Allocation of resources Professional development activities Organizational structures Policy |
| **Side effects** | Practice informed by data Information not always shared | Improved collegiality Formation of partnerships | Improved collegiality, collaboration, and communication Team building Disagreements on process | Improved collegiality, collaboration, and communication Team building Disagreements on process Shared vision |

## Varieties of Action Research

There are four varieties of action research and each variety has some values and own limitations.

1. **Diagnostic.** It is research designed to lead to action. It can be described as research agency steps into an already existing problem situation, preferably by invitation and it thereby, diagnoses the situation.
2. **Participatory.** It grows out the weakness often observed in the first variety. The diagnosis does not always lead to action and that often the main difficulty in securing action stems insufficient community involvement. Its central idea is that the people who are to take action must be involved in the research process from the very beginning. It is a method, which can be used for only a limited range of problems. Thus, it is more a special kind of action techniques than a special kind of research.
3. **Empirical.** The idea behind this variety is to do something and keep a record of what is done and what happens. The research processes are primarily a matter of record – keeping and accumulating experiences in a day work.
4. **Experimental.** It has the greatest potential value for the advances scientific knowledge, since it can provide under favorable circumstance a definitive test of a specific hypothesis.

### Action Research is NOT...

1. It is not the usual things teachers do when they think about their teaching. Action Research is systematic and involves collecting evidence on which to base rigorous reflection.
2. It is not just problem-solving. Action Research involves problem-posing, not just problem-solving. It does not start from a view of problems as incurable ailments. It is motivated by a quest to understand the world by changing it and learning how to improve it from the effects of the changes made.
3. It is not research on other people. Action Research is research by particular people on their own work to help them improve what they do, including how they work with and for others. Action Research does not treat people as objects. It treats people as autonomous, responsible agents who participate actively in making their own histories by knowing what they are doing.
4. It is not the scientific method applied to teaching. Action Research is not just about hypothesis-testing or about using data to come to conclusions. It is concerned with changing situations, not just interpreting them. It brings the researcher into view. Action Research is

a systematically evolving process of changing both the researcher and the situations in which he or she works. The natural and historical sciences do not have this aim.

## Principles of Action Research

The popular assumption is that administrators, mentors, and teachers seek learning strategies and methods to improve the teaching and learning situation in their schools. It is presumed that educators who participate in action research is to have the innate potential to take up/accept challenges that will take place when these new strategies are introduced; want to ensure their own continuous professional development through ongoing Action Research in their institutions and classrooms; and will understand the nature of Action Research, which is different from traditional "academic research."

There are six key principles that help us judge the validity of our action research by linking values, practice, and theory:

1. **Reflective**. Critique Reflecting on issues and processes helps us to become aware of our own ideas and biases. The principle of reflective critique ensures that we reflect on issues and processes and make explicit the interpretations, biases, assumptions, and concerns that formed our judgments. Reflective critique opens our ideas, feelings, thoughts, processes, and conclusions to public review and to self-reflection. By self-reflection and questioning, new arguments can be formed along with the possibility for new actions.
2. **Dialectical Critique**. It is a discussion of different reflective interpretations of practice in order to understand the relationships between all the parts of our environment to see how everything fits together. The key elements to focus attention on are those that are unstable or in opposition to one another. Focusing on these is most likely to create changes.
3. **Collaborative Research**. Co-researchers work together to validate views. Everyone's view is taken into consideration in order to understand the situation better. This principle assumes that every person's ideas are significant, not just those of the Action Researcher. This makes it possible to get insights from the contradictions between the viewpoints of the co-researchers.
4. **Risk.** The change process can cause fears among the researchers. Sometimes it is not easy to hear open discussion of one's interpretations, ideas, and judgments. Action Researchers must be prepared to take a risk by opening their ideas and reflections to criticism and risk failure in order to learn.
5. **Plural Structure.** Reports should contain many (plural) voices reflecting

diverse opinions, comments, and critiques which lead to different interpretations of the evidence (data) and recommendations for different possible actions. Using triangulation in both data-collection and in accounts of the research itself ensures a plural structure. Such a report encourages ongoing discussion among co-researchers, rather than a final conclusion.

6. **Theory, Practice, and Transformation.** Theory and practice are not in opposition in Action Research. They are interdependent and complementary parts of the Action Research change process. They happen together and are both necessary for improvement. The goal of Action Research is to make the theory explicit in order to justify the actions. The application of the theory is then further analyzed in a continuous Action Research cycle that alternates between theory and practice for the process of improvement.

# CHAPTER 2

## WRITING ACTION RESEARCH FROM PROPOSAL TO PRESENTATION

**Learning Competencies**

*At the end of this module, teachers should be able to:*

1. Follow the guidelines and format of action research
2. Identify problems or issues in their classroom and consider possible intervention for them through reflections.
3. Examine the alignment of the identified classroom problems or issues with the Basic Education Research Agenda (BERA)
4. Design and present a good title for an action research topic.
5. Describe the context and rationale of the study.
6. State relevant action research questions.
7. Lists research hypotheses.
8. Indicate scope and limitation of the study.
9. Cite significance of the study.
10. Selects relevant literature
11. Writes coherent review of literature
12. Write proposed innovation, intervention and strategy
13. Choose appropriate research method
14. Describes sampling procedure and the sample.
15. Plans data collection procedure
16. Follow ethical consideration in action research.
17. Plans data analysis using statistics and hypothesis testing.
18. Constructs an instrument and establishes its validity and reliability
19. Collects data using appropriate instruments.
20. Presents and interprets data in tabular and graphical forms.
21. Uses statistical techniques to analyze data— study of differences and relationships limited for bivariate analysis.
22. Draws conclusions from research findings
23. Formulates recommendations
24. Lists references
25. Plan cost estimates/financial reports and work plan
26. Plans for dissemination and advocacy of action research.

## Action Research Proposal

The following template is based from DepEd Order No. 16 s. 2017, Annex 2 Minimum Requirements of the Research Proposal. Teachers in the Basic Education in the Philippines are encouraged to follow and insure that the format is observed before submitting their respective action research proposal to the school research centers and division.

**Action Research Template (DepEd Order no. 16, s. 2017)**

**Title Page**
**Context and Rationale**
- Action Research Questions
- Hypothesis
- Significance of the Study
- Scope and Delimitation

**Literature Review**
- Review of Literature & Studies (Thematic Approach)
- Conceptual -Theoretical Framework

**Proposed Innovation, Intervention, and Strategy**

**Optional Depend on the School Division Format**

**Action Research Methods**
- Types of Research
- Respondents of the Study
- Sample and Sampling Techniques
- Research Instrument
- Data Collection Procedure
- Ethical Consideration
- Data Analysis

**Plans for Dissemination and Advocacy**
**Action Research Methods**
- Types of Research
- Respondents of the Study
- Sample and Sampling Techniques
- Research Instrument
- Data Collection Procedure
- Ethical Consideration
- Data Analysis

**References**
**Appendices**
- Cost Estimates/Financial Reports
- Action / Work Plan
- Sample Research Instruments and table of specification
- Consent and Assent Letter
- Researcher Information
- Declaration of Anti-Plagiarism and Absence of Conflict of Interest

## Criteria for evaluating action research proposal
### The proposal

1. The proposal corresponds with one or more of the listed research priorities;
2. The research proposal is relevant to the problems and needs in the local/national settings in the case of action research.
3. The methodology of the study is justified and sound;
   3.1 well-selected variables
   3.2 clarity of the objectives/problems
   3.3 appropriateness of methodologies
   3.4 comprehensiveness of the review/scanning of literature and empirical studies.
4. The proposal's expected outputs, impacts and derivations are clear and well- defined.
5. The work plan includes a description of each activity in the study including date of completion; and
6. The financial plan and budgetary outlay are adequate and present an itemized breakdown of the total project costs and source/s of funds.

### The Proponent

The proponent has the track record/competence to carry out the proposal research:

1. Academic qualification
2. Research experience in his field of specialization.

## Distinguishing Research Topic, Problem, Purpose and Questions.

The research topic is distinct from the problem of the study, the purpose or intent of the study, and specific research questions. The research problem needs to stand on its own and be recognized as a distinct step because it represents the problem addressed in the study. In the brief definitions that follow, consider the differences among these parts of research:

- A **research topic** is the broad subject matter addressed by the study.
- A **research problem** is a general educational issue, concern, or controversy addressed in research that narrows the topic.
- A **purpose** is the major intent or objective of the study used to address the problem.
- **Research questions** narrow the purpose into specific questions that the researcher would like answered or addressed in the study.

Looking at these differences, you can see that they differ in terms of breadth from broad (topic) to narrow (specific research questions).

Let's examine another example as shown in Figure 2.1, to make this point. In this example, a researcher begins with a broad topic, distance learning. The inquirer then seeks to learn about a problem related to this topic: the lack of students enrolled in distance education classes. To study this problem, our educator then reformulates the problem into a statement of intent (the purpose statement): to study why students do not attend distance education classes at one community college. Examining this statement requires that our investigator narrow the intent to specific questions, one of which is "Does the use of Web site technology in the classroom deter students from enrolling in distance education classes?" The process involves narrowing a broad topic to specific questions. In this process, the "research problem" becomes a distinct step that needs to be identified to help readers clearly see the issue (Creswell, 2012)

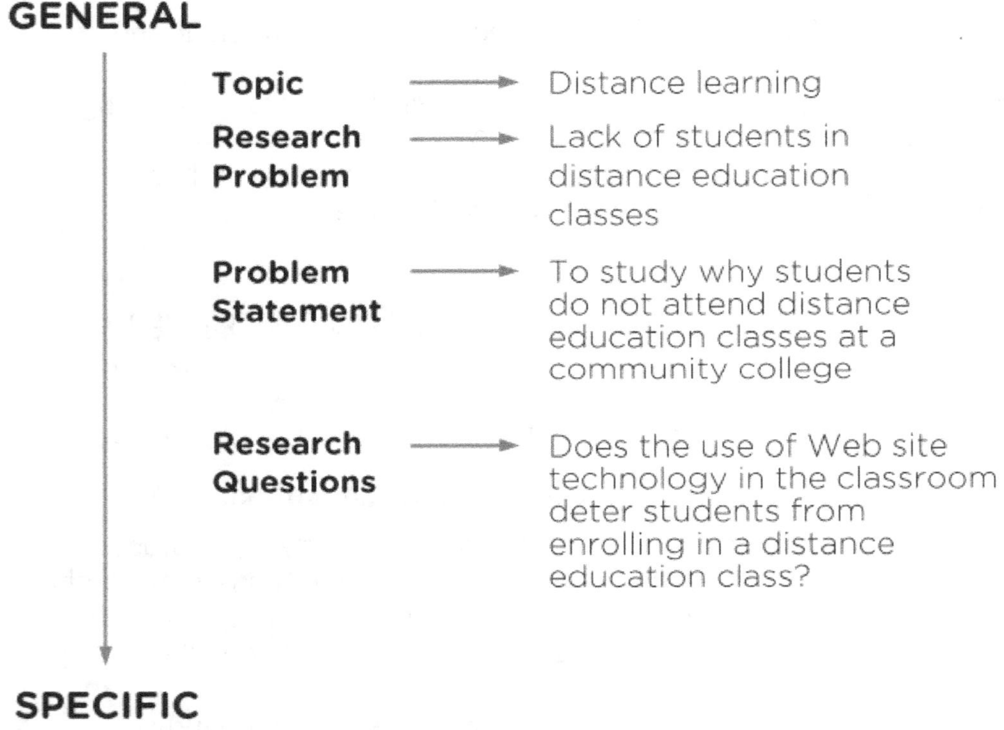


**Figure 2.1 Difference among Research Parts**

## Consideration in Formulating the Action Research Problem

The following are the criteria for choosing an action research problem.

1. **External Criteria**
   a) **Novelty** - this refers to the practical value of the problem due to its "newness" in the field of inquiry.
   b) **Availability of the subjects** - this refers to the people with the desired capability and willingness to participate in the study. The sample of the study participants must be representative enough to ensure reliability and validity of the results.
   c) **Support of the academic community** - this refers to the assistance given by the members of the institution, like the principal, teachers, staff, students, and the parents, in the gathering of data and defraying the cost of the study. Permission of those concerned for the participation in the study of staff members, children the aged, and the mentally challenge should be secured.
   d) **Availability and adequacy of facilities and equipment** - devices such as computer and telephones used in undertaking the study must be considered.
   e) **Ethical consideration** - these include the avoidance of research problems that pose unethical demands on the part of the research participants.

2. **Internal Criteria**
   a) **Experience, training, and qualification of the researcher** - these constitute the researcher's knowledge and expertise as a result of experience and study.
   b) **Motivation, interest, intellectual curiosity, and perceptiveness of the researcher** - these are essential attitudes that bring anticipated satisfaction or enjoyment in the completion of research tasks.
   c) **Time - Factor** - this considers the fact that studies must be pursued within a given time frame.
   d) **Costs and returns** - these factors matter in choosing a research problem. Research is an expensive undertaking. The amount of funding needed, after all, depends on the size of the sample, the place where the research is to be conducted, the treatment of data, and the kind of research design.
   e) **Hazards, penalties, and handicaps** - these depends upon the researcher's physical and intellectual capacity and moral judgment.

## The Research Agenda

Proceed by saying: “Considering the problems or issues that you have identified and reflected upon, let us now see if we can align these with the Action Research themes identified in the Basic Education Research Agenda (BERA) of the Department of Education (DepEd). These themes were formulated to help teachers generate Action Research topics.” The BERA is a document containing a list of priority education research areas to guide DepEd and its stakeholders in the conduct of research. In the case of teacher- researchers, selecting a research focus begins with asking “What education research themes are related to the problems or issues I have encountered?”

## BERA Research Themes:

**The following are the themes listed in the BERA.**

1. **Teaching and Learning.** This research theme covers the actors, activities, and fundamental aspects of teaching and learning in various contexts.
2. **Child Protection.** This research theme focuses on incidents of child abuse such as bullying, teenage pregnancy, addictive behaviors, and child labor.
3. **Human Resource Development.** This research theme includes studies on the vast human capital involved in delivering basic education such as teaching and non-teaching personnel, hiring qualifications, career development, and employee welfare.
4. **Governance.** This research theme encompasses planning, finance, program management, transparency and accountability, and evaluation. It underscores DepEd’s commitment to ensure that its structure, systems, and processes contribute to the achievement of basic education outcomes.

## Cross-Cutting Themes:

1. **Disaster Risk Reduction and Management (DRRM).** This research theme focuses on disaster prevention and mitigation, preparedness, response, and rehabilitation and recovery.
2. **Gender and Development (GAD).** This research theme includes studies on gender mainstreaming and gender responsiveness of DepEd structures, policies, programs, and projects.
3. **Inclusive Education.** This research theme involves the perceptions and readiness of the department in providing an inclusive learning environment.

**The following are the possible topics under each research theme:**

1. **Teaching and Learning**
    a) classroom assessment (e.g., formative and summative)
    b) emerging good practices
    c) teachers' expertise in constructing various types of assessments
    d) availability of assessment tools and resources (e.g., materials, manpower, environment, portfolio assessments),
    e) continuing professional development and support (e.g., coaching and mentoring, LAC)
    f) medium of instruction
    g) ICT integration in teaching strategies in teaching
    h) classroom management differentiated instruction
2. **Child Protection**
    a) bullying (physical, emotional, and cyber)
    b) reproductive health education
    c) child abuse (grave child rights violation, SHS work immersion context)
    d) addiction (substance abuse, online gaming, social media)
    e) media consumption (internet, TV and film, magazines, radio)
3. **Human Resource Development**
    a) teaching specialization
    b) language proficiency (MTB-MLE)
    c) academic skills and psychosocial skill
    d) ICT integration in teaching
    e) interpersonal skills
    f) teacher induction program
    g) work performance of teachers and incentives
    h) gender and development
4. **Governance**
    a) process/tools (typologies and classification, comprehensive DRRM)
    b) Water, Sanitation, and Hygiene Programs (WASH)
    c) health and nutrition d data management
    d) partnerships
5. **Disaster Risk Reduction and Management (DRRM)**
    a) disaster prevention and mitigation
    b) disaster preparedness
    c) disaster response
    d) disaster rehabilitation and recovery.
6. **Gender and Development (GAD)**
    a) gender mainstreaming
    b) gender responsiveness
7. **Inclusive Education**

a) perceptions on inclusive education
b) readiness in providing an inclusive learning environment.

## Generating Research Topics through Reflection

Reflection requires going beyond merely thinking about experiences. It is expected that reflecting on problems and issues in your classrooms will lead to action on your part. Reflection-for-action is thinking about experiences and planning for future action (Hendricks 2006). In conducting Action Research, the teacher initiates a process of solving a specific problem or issue in his or her practice. The process involves problem-solving implemented by practitioners, working independently or with others in teams, to address concerns or issues and improve instruction and learning.

Samosa (2022) enumerated that role of reflection in action research is to create models from a body of previous knowledge and to reframe a problem or issue; then interventions are carried out which lead to outcomes which are analyzed further. From this, reflection is a tool for promoting actions, and it is intended to lead to actions which promote improved educational practices. Through reflection it enhances the iterative and investigative nature of action research.

## Principles of Reflective Practice in Action Research

The following are the reflective practices in doing action research.

1. It needs to be understood as a set of meanings, statements, stories, etc., which produce a particular version of events. This reflective discourse – or conversation – is at the heart of the improvement process.
2. It is fueled and energized by experience. Reflecting on something is our experience and all that it comprises. Reflecting on experience is a way of interrogating our actions and thinking in particular ways.
3. It means returning to re-look at our taken-for-granted values, professional understanding and practices. It is not about reflecting on the extraordinary; it is about the ordinary, everyday occurrences of the working day. In this 'reflective turn' we consider the parts played by ourselves and others in these occurrences so that we may deepen our understanding of them.
4. It is about learning to explain and justify the way we go about things.
5. It means considering what we do 'problematically' – by constantly inquiring and questioning what we do systematically so that we may learn continuously from it.
6. It means putting what we know and learn to use, and informing improvement – by doing something positive and constructive through the

knowledge we create which is purposeful. Engaging in thinking around what interests will be served through this process is important.

7. It means applying critical thinking to practice by asking probing or challenging questions, both of self and collectively so that transformation can take place.
8. It is a way of decoding the symbolic landscape around us – for example, why an environment is equipped in the way that it is, the way in which human relations occur, what appears significant or worthy within the environment, and the way in which these things are responded to. Symbolism is an important element in the reflective discourse.
9. It is a linkage between theoretical knowledge and practical application, enabling practitioners to create meaningful theories of action that are live and real.
10. It is eclectic, and is comfortable with drawing on different ways of knowing. It is not prejudiced in how knowledge is gained or understood and acts as an intersection between different approaches.

**Writing Action Research Title**

After the selection of the theme or the topic to write on, the action researcher considers the title of the action research and what criterion measures exists for presenting a good one. Among the different considerations for this action is the following:

1. It should not be long and should not be more than 20 words.
2. It should include the variables (independent and dependent) of the study.
3. It should give insight virtually on what the research is all about.
4. It should serve as reference for the whole research report which others can use.
5. It should enable one to claim the paper as his own; and helps other researchers to refers to ones' work as they survey some theories themselves.
6. The title is reflective of the main objective or the salient findings of the study.
7. It lends international character especially when the paper is intended for international journal publication.
8. It indicates the subject of the study as well as its scope.
9. It stimulates the interest of the readers.
10. It utilizes the current taxonomy (or word choice) from the field of study.
11. It ignores redundant phrases or wasteful words such as "An investigation of," "An analysis of," "A study of on," or similar constructions.
12. It may be crafted in declarative or interrogative statement.
13. It is written out with the letter of the first word capitalized, including that of the first word of a subtitle. All content words (nouns, verbs, adjectives, and

adverbs) that come in between the first word and last word of the title are also capitalized.

14. The title can be crafted creatively.
15. It is written creatively satisfying the typical function – to explore and/or explain a world phenomenon of a qualitative action research. In some instances, a subtitle is used along with the main title. It functions in the following ways (Samosa, 2022):
    a) It provides explication or explanation.
    b) It enhances a main title (oftentimes in direct quote) which is literacy, if not, imaginative.
    c) It contextualizes the research.
    d) It describes the temporal or progressive scope of the study.
    e) It reflects or identifies the research method or approach used.

## Noticing Spots in Empirical Research

It is important when writing about action research to get clear about the difference between research that is adequate, inadequate and research that is partial.

There are four concepts that are helpful in deciding which of these is the case. These are:

1. **Blind spots**. those topics that we 'don't know well enough to even ask about or care about. These are the things, the method, definitions or theoretical approach does not allow to be seen/said. For example, surveys are very good for answering questions such as how many, and how often. They are not very good at probing the reasons why this may be the case. Conversely, a small number of case studies may allow you to build really rich descriptions but does not allow you to generalize to scale.
2. **Bald spots**. Those topics that are repeatedly pursued in research.
3. **Blank spots.** Those topics about which 'we know enough to question, but not to answer. These are the things that are not yet covered by this study. All studies have a particular scope, location, are conducted at a particular time, in a particular context and with particular people and things. there are therefore plenty of other circumstances which the research does not cover. These things-not-covered constitute blank spots.
4. **Bright spots.** Those topics that inspire and innovate research.

## Writing the Introduction (Context and Rationale) of Action Research

The introduction is important in establishing the cognitive setting of the research (Cristobal & Cristobal, 2013). The introduction explains why this research is important or necessary or important. Begin by describing the problem or situation that motivates the research. Move to discussing the current state of research in the field; then reveal a "gap" or problem in the field. Finally, explain how the present research is a solution to that problem or gap. More so, it has the following elements:

1. Rationalization of the need to research on the problem;
2. Clarification of the important terminologies for the reader to easily understand what the research is about and
3. Establishment of the degree of seriousness of the problem which prompted the researcher to look for solutions

The following questions will aid the researcher in formulating the introduction.

1. **What is the rationale of the problem?** This question is answered by sharing the reasons why the researcher decided to look for solutions to the problem. A rationale may include the narration of personal experiences, a description of an article read, a scene witnessed, a news heard, or a theory that needs to be clarified. The researcher should describe the existing and prevailing problem based on his or her experience. The scope may be local, national, or international. Ideally, the rationale can start from a global perspective to a more personal one.
2. **What is the setting of the problem?** The setting forms part of the delimitation of the study. It defines the geographic boundaries and certain demographic characteristics of the research. This describes the place where the research was conducted, since the setting has a significant bearing on the variables being studied. In the description of the setting, its distinctive characteristics must be highlighted.

3. **What is the basic literature foundation of the study?** This is different from the review of the related theories, conceptual literature, and research literature. This part seeks to provide the researcher clarity on the terms or variables used in the study. The terms and variables must be clear to the researcher for an easy understanding of the readers. As such, sufficient background can assist the investigator in determining the boundaries of the study. This part is derived from different literature sources. The use of various references is crucial in this part of the first chapter.
4. **How serious is the chosen research problem?** The researcher is tasked to identify the intensity and magnitude of the problem. When the gravity of the problem has already been described, he or she may then gauge the kind of action to be used to identify the problem. In most cases, the researcher at this point looks for statistical or quantitative evidence to assess the significance of the problem at hand.
5. **What is the general objective of the problem?** This is the general statement of the problem or the major tasks of the researcher to discharge and should also be the basis of the enumerated statements of specific problems.
6. **What is the overall purpose of the problem?** It is important to note that the

researcher must be totally aware of the purpose of the research problem. He or she must fully understand the implications of the resulting findings of the study.

**Illustrative Example of Context and Rationale:**

**Reframing Remote Learning Assessment Practices of Teachers': Input for School- Based Testing Reforms (Samosa, 2022)**

**CONTEXT AND RATIONALE**

**Introduction**

As schools around the world have closed due to coronavirus (COVID-19) pandemic students, teachers, and parents are settling into the "new reality" for the foreseeable future. Many schools are implementing their distance learning contingency plans and connecting students and teachers through online platforms and tools. National and local governments are partnering with broadcasting service providers to deliver educational content via television and radio during dedicated hours. Under these unexpected circumstances, teachers and parents have had to quickly adapt to teaching in this new reality to ensure that students engage in learning.

In response to this crisis and to ensure the continuity of learning while assuring the health, safety, and well-being of all learners, teachers, and other employees. the Department of Education instituted DepEd Order No.12 series of 2020 to establish new learning delivery modalities in all levels embodied in the Learning Continuity Plan (LCP) for the school year 2020-2021. The alternative modes of delivering learning were envisioned to reach all learners regardless of who and where they are. Among these implemented learning delivery modalities (LDMs) were Distance Learning, Blended Learning, and Homeschooling. The Department of Education (DepEd) conducted Learning Enrollment and Survey Form (LESF) on school opening (Department of Education, 2020), it was found out that Modular learning, a form of distance learning that uses Self-Learning Modules (SLM) is one of the highly convenient for most of the typical Filipino students. It was also the most preferred learning system of the majority of parents/guardians for their children. The SLM is based on the most essential learning competencies (MELCS) provided by the Department of Education.

**Rationale of the problem**

However, without the grasp of the teacher and authentic learning experiences as in face-to-face teaching-learning process, the learners will have a difficulty in understanding the topic and will be demotivated to learn ultimately leading to the submission of incomplete answers in the modules or totally non-submission of modules resulting to poor academic performance and a risk of failure of the students. On the survey conducted by the Graceville National High School's Research Unit. Out of 45 students in a section, an average of 13 learners passed an incomplete answer in module and 8 learners did not passed the module at all on a weekly submission of modules.

This also indicates that those learners will have a failing grade if not treated with an intervention and remediation.

**Seriousness of the Problem**

In line with the Global Education Monitoring Report (2020) expressed issues in educational aspects, one of which is on assessment practices. Classroom assessment has been a topic of interest for researchers in the new normal of education owing to lack of preparation superimposed with the inherent problems of remote assessment. The main challenges identified in remote assessment were academic dishonesty, infrastructure, coverage of learning outcomes, and commitment of learners to submit assessments (Laitusis, 2020). Focusing on assessment is important for the development of teaching and learning processes. Assessment enables teachers and students to draw inferences from the information obtained and act accordingly. Such actions may aid in making the necessary improvements to teaching and learning, or simply provide a picture in time of students' competence or achievement (Black and Wiliam, 2018).

**Literature Foundation**

In a way it is observed that the teachers develop new alternative and varied approaches to monitor learners' learning from assessing to remediating learning losses during the COVID-19 crisis, including both formative and summative methods. Different methods may be required per grade and subject area for both individual and collective feedback and support. Moreover, teachers may lack relevant resources at home, training and experience, particularly on distance learning platform. Some programmes may largely reduce the amount of time allocated to teacher-directed learning processes by focusing on learners' self-learning. Upon return to school, teachers may also struggle to assess learners' learning levels to identify whether learners are on track, and any learning gaps or losses resulting from the school closure and for remedial actions. Such assessments may be critical in informing learning process and/or students' promotion, certification and access to higher levels of education.

From this, learner cannot and should not be expected to learn and progress across the intended curriculum through self-learning methods with few interactions from teachers. Distance learning modalities should integrate a formative and summative assessment component, whereby students submit work to teachers and teachers provide individualized and/or collective feedback regarding learning content and student error patterns. This can be established through complementary communication elements between teachers and students (e.g. teachers checking in on students via mobile) or integrate a role for parents as facilitators. Expectations for formative and summative assessment need to be clearly communicated to schools, teachers, learners and parents. Teachers may use various channels to collect and assess learners' work regarding learning areas targets and priorities: online platforms can be used, homework can be dropped off at a given location on a given day, according to local regulations or teachers can contact learners' periodically. Protocols should be put in place when learners are identified as not learning or not accessing distance learning modality.

**Setting of the Problem**

As regards how assessment practices are currently being reshaped in the Philippine Basic Education, the Department of Education (DepEd) issued DepEd Order No. 31, s. 2020 or the Interim Guidelines for Assessment and Grading in Light of the Basic Education Learning Continuity Plan. This is to provide guidance on the assessment of student learning and on the grading scheme for school year 2020-2021, which are key to understanding and addressing gaps in education among students that pursues learning continuity for schools to take stock of assessment and grading practices that are more meaningfully support learner development and respond to varied contexts at this time. More so, the learners' assessment should be holistic and authentic in capturing the attainment of the most essential learning competencies.

**General objective of the problem**

With all this information, the researcher was prompted to conduct this study since it was observed that the learners at risk in achieving and mastering the most essential learning competencies in the remote learning. This research led to evaluate the present assessment practice on the remote learning as the basis to reform the school-based testing program based on the findings of the study.

**Overall purpose of the problem**

## Writing Action Research Problem

The problem is the heart of any research project. Without a focused research problem, there is no research. More so, it will be difficult any research unless a clear problem is initially stated. Statement of the problem states the purpose of the study and clarify various essential elements of research such as the major variables, the general and specific objectives, and the appropriate methodology. This should be in consonance with the research title. The opening paragraph of this part of action research paper contains the general problem of the study. It has to be restated with specific details on the participants, setting, and period of study. The following are important elements in the statement of the general problems are:

1. **Main tasks**. They satisfy the question, "what to do the major variables such as to associate, to relate, to assess, to measure, to determine, etc.
2. **Main or major variables**.
3. **Participants. subjects or respondents**
4. **The specific setting**
5. **Coverage date of the conduct of study**.

6. For developmental research and action research, the **intended output** such as an intervention program, innovation, module, policies, among others.

Samosa (2021), elucidated that statement of the action research problem has two main elements.

1. **The General Action Research Objective** - is the first part of the problem where the action researcher states the objectives. This is a statement of a long - term objective expected to be achieved by the study. This is derived by the identification and crystallization of the research problem and as reflected in the title.
2. **Action Research Questions** - identifies the problem (s) which will be addressed by the research in terms of investigating or testing an idea; trying out solutions to a problem; creating a new procedure or system; explaining a phenomenon; or a combination of any of these (DepEd Order No. 43, s. 2015).

**Illustrative Example of Action Research Problem**

**Reframing Remote Learning Assessment Practices of Teachers': Input for School- Based Testing Reforms (Samosa, 2022)**

**Action Research Problem/Questions**

This study evaluates the assessment practice of teachers on the remote learning in Graceville National High, Schools Division of San Jose de Monte Bulacan in the in new normal situation which serves as the basis to reform the school-based testing program during the LAC and In-Service Training. Specifically, this research seeks to answer the following questions:

**General Action Research Objective**

1. What is the profile of the teacher-respondents be described in terms of?
   1.1 Age
   1.2 Gender
   1.3 Areas of Specialization
   1.4 Years of teaching,
   1.5 Highest Educational Attainment
   1.6 Training Attended?
2. What is the level of teacher's competence and practice on the remote learning assessment in terms of the following component:

2.1 Competencies on remote learning assessment
   2.1.1 Assessment Occurring Prior to Instruction.
   2.1.2 Assessment Occurring During Instruction.
   2.1.3 Assessment Occurring After the Appropriate Instructional Segment
2.2 Level of assessment practices
   2.2.1 clarity of assessment
   2.2.2 time and effort on task
   2.2.3 quality of feedback
   2.2.4 motivational belief and self-esteem to learners
   2.2.5 interaction and dialogue about learning progress
   2.2.6 self- assessment and reflection of learning of the learners
   2.2.7 assessment – content and process in adapting teaching to students needs

3. Is there a significant difference in the assessment of the teacher- respondents on the level of competencies on the remote learning assessment when grouped according to profile?
4. Is there a significant difference in the assessment of the teacher- respondents on the Level of assessment practices when grouped according to profile?
5. What are the challenges encountered by the teacher respondents on the remote learning assessment?

**Action Research Questions**

## Classification of Research Questions

a) **Factor - isolating question** – it ask the question "what is this?" these questions are sometimes called factor - naming question because they isolate, categorize, describe, or name factors and situations.

**Mobile Virtual Laboratory as Innovative Strategy to Improve Learners' Achievement, Attitudes, and Learning Environment in Teaching Chemistry (Samosa, 2021)**

1. What is the attitude of the learners as exposed to the mobile virtual laboratory as innovative strategy in teaching chemistry as described in the following?
   1.1 Inquiry
   1.2 Enjoyment
2. What is the level of learners' learning environment during the mobile virtual laboratory as innovative strategy in teaching chemistry as described in the following?
   2.1 Integration

2.2 Material Environment
2.3 Teacher Support
2.4 Task Orientation
2.5 Investigation
2.6 Differentiation

b) **Factor - relating questions** - these ask the question 'what is happening here?" The goals of this question are to determine the relationship among factors that have been identified.

**CoSIM (Comics cum SIM): An Innovative Material in Teaching Biology (Samosa, 2021)**

Is there significant relationship between the level of academic performance and the attitudes towards exposure to CoSIM?

c) **Situation - relating questions** - these questions ask the question "what will happen if...? These questions usually yield hypotheses testing or experimental study design in which the researcher manipulates the variables the variables to see what will happen.

**Effectiveness of Claim, Evidence and Reasoning as An Innovation to Develop Students' Scientific Argumentative Writing Skills (Samosa, 2021)**

Is there a significance difference between the pretest and posttest scores of the students' scientific argumentative writing skills that was exposed to C-E-R innovation?

d) **Situation – producing questions** - these questions asks the question "how can I make it happen?" these questions establish explicit goals for action, develop plans or prescriptions to achieve goals, and specify the conditions under which these goals will be accomplished.

**Virtual Laboratory as Self-paced Learning Innovation to Improve Learners' Achievement and Attitude in Teaching Physical Science (Samosa, et.al, 2022)**

What lesson exemplar in science virtual laboratory may be developed based on the finding of the study?

## Hypothesis

Based on the specific research problems, hypothesis is formulated. The hypothesis is a tentative but intelligent and logical guess/answer to a specific question/problem which is carefully formulated before conducting the study. it predicts the outcome of an action research study.

A good hypothesis provides direction to a study. It enables the action researcher to formulate the conclusion (s) of the research work. The results of the study are the basis for its acceptance or rejection at the end of the study. A good hypothesis must be briefly and clearly stated. It should also be worded in such a way that is would be easy for the reader to remember it throughout reading the entire action research paper.

The following are the characteristics of a good hypothesis in action research:

1. It can be empirically tested.
2. It should state in definite terms the relationship between the variables under study.
3. It is based on the question raised in the action research study and is stated in such a way that it logically answer the question.
4. It is based on findings of previous studies
5. It is related to a body of theory.

## Categories of Hypotheses

There are two of hypothesis:

1. The **null hypothesis ($H_0$)** is a statement of "no significant difference" or of "no significant relationship between two or more variables or groups that are to be measured and tested through inferential statistics". It is stated in the negative form so it could be treated statistically.
2. The **alternative hypothesis** ($H_1$) is the type of hypothesis which affirms of the existence of observed phenomenon and is the opposite of the null hypothesis because the former is stated in positive form.

## Form of Alternative Hypothesis

1. The **directional hypothesis ($H_1$)** the action researcher makes prediction about the expected outcome. Basing this prediction on prior literature and studies on the topic that suggest a potential outcome. For example, the action researcher may predict that scores will be higher for Group A than Group B" on the dependent variable or that "Group A will change more than Group B" on the outcome. These examples illustrate a directional hypothesis because an expected prediction (e.g., higher, more change) is made.

2. The **non – directional hypothesis** it is a prediction is made, but the exact form of differences (e.g., higher, lower, more, less) is not specified because the action researcher does not know what can be predicted from past literature. Thus, the action researcher might write, "There is a difference" between the two group.

**Illustrative Example of Action Research Hypothesis**

> **Mobile Physics as Innovation to Reinvigorating Active Engagement and Learning Dynamics of Grade 11 Learners on Uniform Accelerated Motion (Samosa, 2021)**
>
> **Hypothesis**
>
> This study tested the null hypothesis, which subjected to a statistical test at α 0.05 level of significance:
>
> **$H_0$:** There is no significant difference that exists between the pre-test and post-test results of using mobile physics s on teaching uniform accelerated motion.

## Scope and delimitation of the study

This includes the coverage of the action research study area, the subjects, the research instrument, the research issues and concerns, the duration of the study, and the constrains that have direct bearing the result of the studies.

A scope addresses how a study will be narrowed, and how it is bounded. This is the place to explain the things that you are not doing and why you have chosen not to do them. In here, the researcher gives reasons why a particular literature will not be reviewed, the population you are not studying, the methodological procedures you will not use. Limit your discussion of scope to the things that a reader might reasonably expect you to do but that you, for clearly explained reasons, have decided not to do. The scope usually includes the general problem to be investigated including the time frame or work.

A limitation identifies potential weakness of the study. In doing this, try to consider the nature of self-report, instrument used, and the sample or the respondents involved in the study as well as some threats to internal validity that maybe impossible to avoid or minimize. Looking on the difference between limitation and delimitation of the study, Limitation of the study indicates the variables that are to be contained/studied in the action research, while delimitation of the study is those which are not part (excluded) of the study.

The scope and limitations of the study may be defined in context and content. Contentwise defines scope in terms of the different aspects or areas specified in the statement of the action research problems, while contextwise defines the scope in terms of the period covered, the focus subject or inquiry and the place where the research will be conducted.

In writing this section, the first paragraph should contain the scope(s) and the second paragraph should have the limitation(s) of the studyMore so, the following are the consideration in discussing the scope and limitation of the study.

1. How have you narrowed the scope of the study?
2. Did you focus only on selected aspects of the problem, certain areas of interest, a limited range of subjects, or particular level of ability?
3. What are the limitations surrounding your study within which conclusions must be confined?
4. What limitation exist in your research methodology?

## Illustrative Example of Scope and limitations of the study

**Cultivating Research Culture: Capacity Building Program Toward Initiatives to Improve Teachers Self-efficacy, Research Anxiety and Research attitude (Samosa, 2021)**

This study determined the effectiveness of capacity building program towards research initiatives to improve the teachers' level of research self-efficacy, research anxiety and research attitude among the Faculty members of Graceville National High School. The respondents of this study were the fifty (50) public secondary teachers composed of nine (9) Senior High School Teachers and forty - one (41) Junior High School Teachers in Graceville National High School. Teachers included in the study as respondents were purposively chosen. The teacher-respondents will be undergone a series of webinar on crafting action research proposal and presentation during school learning action cell.

For a deeper analysis of the main problem, a significant relationship between research self-efficacy, research anxiety, and research attitude towards research initiative in conducting action research and the profile of novice teachers – researchers, significant difference in the assessment of capacity building program for action research when novice teachers – researchers group according to profile and there a significant relationship among research self-efficacy, research anxiety and research attitude among novice teachers – researchers were taken into consideration.

The data were gathered through standardized survey questionnaires from the study of Rezai and Zamani-Miandashti (2015). Then, the data were treated statistically using percentage and frequency distribution, weighted mean, Analysis of variance (ANOVA), Chi-square test and adapted research culture index from the study of Barroso and Egar (2015).

## Significance of the Study

As a scholarly undertaking, an action research writing has to place a premium on its possible original contribution to knowledge as one of its most possible original contribution to knowledge as one of the its most important objectives. In fact, it is what distinguishes it from other academic studies. The new knowledge obtained by the researcher in an action research must be related to existing theories, used in new products, standards, protocols, procedures or other information and applied to professional practices for improvement of both the discipline and the profession. The significance of the study specifies the individuals, stakeholders or groups to use and be benefited by the knowledge or information obtained from research and how the study is able to contribute to the discipline and the profession. In may also specify the contribution of the study to the educational practices, teaching and learning. It is the section where one can observe that the researcher generalizes beyond the objective data gathered in the course of research. It is where the researcher suggests the uses, functions and importance of findings of the study.

In short, the researcher must state in the significance of the study, particularly the importance and relevance of the outcomes of the study to the discipline, profession, its clients and the people in general. The outcome could be:

a) the acquisition of new knowledge;
b) the development of new theories or knowledge, paradigms, and
c) the transformation of the whole knowledge paradigms.

The study must serve or include one or more of following purposes of research:

a) to build a body of objective knowledge;
b) to facilitate and enhance practice;
c) to contribute to knowledge economy, and
d) to improve the quality of life.

This section discusses the importance of the results of the research study to all concerned, particularly the beneficiaries of the research such as to:

a) an individual or group of individuals,
b) stake holders,
c) the government,
d) society or a specific community,
e) the agency and institution,
f) the international community,
g) the profession,
h) the action research writer himself, and
i) the future researchers.

The significance of the study answers or addresses how the study will affect or impact on the lives of these people and their sectoral performance. It emphasizes the probable utilization, positive effect and impact of the study and its contribution to practice, research, education and administration. The contribution to knowledge, as said earlier, whether in theory or practice, must not only pertain to knowledge per se, but knowledge economy, national and even global development.

## Illustrative Example of Significance of the Study

**Online – Merge – Offline (OMO) Classroom Model as Innovation to Improve Students' Mastery Level and Attitude in Teaching Balancing Chemical Equation (Samosa, et al., 2021)**

**Significance of the Study**

The outcome of this study give understanding to educators in general and to researchers, school administrator, parents, students and science teachers. More specifically, the researchers believe that the findings of this study serve the following purpose.

**Learners.** This study could provide information for the appropriate learning strategy in Teaching Balancing Chemical Equation that would be reflective to the needs of the learner. The findings may help the learners to improve their knowledge and skills and can lead to a better understanding and mastery of the certain learning area.

**Teachers**. The result of this study can add to the teachers understanding of Online – Merge – Offline (OMO) Classroom Model which the teachers already using and suggest new ways to use in the teaching learning process.

**School Administrators**. This serves as a guide in designing and conducting teachers training/in-service training. This increases the supervisory strategies that will help take an action in the teaching-learning areas in the school and the curriculum itself.

**Academic Researchers**. This study may help as a guide to academic researchers and provide insights that will serve as basis for future studies. From the output of this study, they may come up new ideas and strategies in the field of education.

## Literature Review

A literature review is a piece of academic writing demonstrating knowledge and understanding of the academic literature on a specific topic placed in context. A literature review also includes a critical evaluation of the material; this is why it is called a literature review rather than a literature report (Institute for Academic Development, 2021). More so, it compiles and evaluates the research available on a certain topic or issue that you are researching and writing about.

**Importance of a Good Literature Review (Jesson, 2011)**

A literature review may consist of simply a summary of key sources, but in the social sciences, a literature review usually has an organizational pattern and combines both summary and synthesis, often within specific conceptual categories. A summary is a recap of the important information of the source, but a synthesis is a re-organization, or a reshuffling, of that information in a way that informs how you are planning to investigate a research problem. The analytical features of a literature review might:

1. Give a new interpretation of old material or combine new with old interpretations;
2. Trace the intellectual progression of the field, including major debates;
3. Depending on the situation, evaluate the sources and advise the reader on the most pertinent or relevant research, or
4. Usually in the conclusion of a literature review, identify where gaps exist in how a problem has been researched to date.

**The purpose of a literature review (Ridley, 2012).**

1. Place each work in the context of its contribution to understanding the research problem being studied.
2. Describe the relationship of each work to the others under consideration.
3. Identify new ways to interpret prior research.
4. Reveal any gaps that exist in the literature.
5. Resolve conflicts amongst seemingly contradictory previous studies.
6. Identify areas of prior scholarship to prevent duplication of effort.
7. Point the way in fulfilling a need for additional research.
8. Locate your own research within the context of existing literature.

**Types of Literature Reviews**

Literature reviews are designed to provide an overview of sources the researcher has explored while researching a particular topic and to demonstrate to the readers how the research fits within a larger field of study. The following are the basic types of literature review:

1. **Narrative literature review.** critiques the literature and summarizes the body of a literature. Narrative review also draws conclusions about the topic

and identifies gaps or inconsistencies in a body of knowledge. You need to have a sufficiently focused research question to conduct a narrative literature review.

2. **Systematic literature**. review requires more rigorous and well-defined approach compared to most other types of literature review. Systematic literature review is comprehensive and details the timeframe within which the literature was selected. Systematic literature review can be divided into two categories: meta-analysis and meta-synthesis. When you conduct meta-analysis, you take findings from several studies on the same subject and analyze these using standardized statistical procedures. In meta-analysis patterns and relationships are detected and conclusions are drawn. Meta-analysis is associated with deductive research approach.

   Meta-synthesis, on the other hand, is based on non-statistical techniques. This technique integrates, evaluates and interprets findings of multiple qualitative research studies. Meta-synthesis literature review is conducted usually when following inductive research.
3. **Argumentative literature review**. as the name implies, examines literature selectively in order to support or refute an argument, deeply imbedded assumption, or philosophical problem already established in the literature. It should be noted that a potential for bias is a major shortcoming associated with argumentative literature review.
4. **Integrative literature review.** It reviews, critiques, and synthesizes secondary data about research topic in an integrated way such that new frameworks and perspectives on the topic are generated. If your research does not involve primary data collection and data analysis, then using integrative literature review will be your only option.
5. **Theoretical literature review** focuses on a pool of theory that has accumulated in regard to an issue, concept, theory, phenomena. Theoretical literature reviews play an instrumental role in establishing what theories already exist, the relationships between them, to what degree the existing theories have been investigated, and to develop new hypotheses to be tested.
6. **Methodological Review**. A review does not always focus on what someone said [content], but how they said it [method of analysis]. This approach provides a framework of understanding at different levels (i.e. those of theory, substantive fields, research approaches and data collection and analysis techniques), enables researchers to draw on a wide variety of knowledge ranging from the conceptual level to practical documents for use in fieldwork in the areas of ontological and epistemological consideration, quantitative and qualitative integration, sampling, interviewing, data collection and data analysis, and helps highlight many ethical issues which we should be aware of and consider as we go through our study.

**Literature Review Organization**

1. **Chronological.** If your review follows the chronological method, you could write about the materials according to when they were published. This approach should only be followed if a clear path of research building on previous research can be identified and that these trends follow a clear chronological order of development.
2. **By Publication.** Order your sources by publication chronology, then, only if the order demonstrates a more important trend. For instance, you could order a review of literature on environmental studies of brown fields if the progression revealed, for example, a change in the soil collection practices of the researchers who wrote and/or conducted the studies.
3. **Thematic (conceptual categories).** Thematic reviews of literature are organized around a topic or issue, rather than the progression of time. However, progression of time may still be an important factor in a thematic review. The only difference here between a "chronological" and a "thematic" approach is what is emphasized the most. Note however that more authentic thematic reviews tend to break away from chronological order. A review organized in this manner would shift between time periods within each section according to the point made.
4. **Methodological.** A methodological approach focuses on the methods utilized by the researcher.

**Writing Your Literature Review**

Once you have settled on how to organize your literature review, you are ready to write each section. When writing your review, keep in mind these issues.

1. **Use Evidence**. A literature review section is, in this sense, just like any other academic research paper. Your interpretation of the available sources must be backed up with evidence that demonstrates that what you are saying is valid.
2. **Be Selective.** Select only the most important points in each source to highlight in the review. The type of information you choose to mention should relate directly to the research problem, whether it is thematic, methodological, or chronological. Related items that provide additional information but that are not key to understanding the research problem can be included in a list of further readings.
3. **Use Quotes Sparingly.** Some short quotes are okay if you want to emphasize a point, or if what an author stated cannot be easily paraphrased. Sometimes you may need to quote certain terminology that was coined by the author, not common knowledge, or taken directly from

the study. Do not use extensive quotes as a substitute for your own summary and interpretation of the literature.

4. **Summarize and Synthesize.** Remember to summarize and synthesize your sources within each thematic paragraph as well as throughout the review. Recapitulate important features of a research study, but then synthesize it by rephrasing the study's significance and relating it to your own work.
5. **Keep Your Own Voice.** While the literature review presents others' ideas, your voice [the writer's] should remain front and center. For example, weave references to other sources into what you are writing but maintain your own voice by starting and ending the paragraph with your own ideas and wording.
6. **Use Caution When Paraphrasing.** When paraphrasing a source that is not your own, be sure to represent the author's information or opinions accurately and in your own words. Even when paraphrasing an author's work, you still must provide a citation to that work.

**Common Mistakes to Avoid in Writing Literature Review.**

These are the most common mistakes made in reviewing literature.

1. Sources in your literature review do not clearly relate to the research problem;
2. You do not take sufficient time to define and identify the most relevant sources to use in the literature review related to the research problem;
3. Relies exclusively on secondary analytical sources rather than including relevant primary research studies or data;
4. Uncritically accepts another researcher's findings and interpretations as valid, rather than examining critically all aspects of the research design and analysis.
5. Does not describe the search procedures that were used in identifying the literature to review;
6. Reports isolated statistical results rather than synthesizing them in chi-squared or meta-analytic methods; and,
7. Only includes research that validates assumptions and does not consider contrary findings and alternative interpretations found in the literature.

**Parts of Literature Review**

Most lit reviews use a basic introduction-body-conclusion structure; if your lit review is part of a larger paper, the introduction and conclusion pieces may be just a few sentences while you focus most of your attention on the body. If your lit review is a standalone piece, the introduction and conclusion take up more space and give you a place to discuss your goals, research methods, and conclusions separately from where you discuss the literature itself.

1. **Introduction.**
   a) An introductory paragraph that explains what your working topic and thesis is
   b) A forecast of key topics or texts that will appear in the review.
   c) Potentially, a description of how you found sources and how you analyzed them for inclusion and discussion in the review (more often found in published, standalone literature reviews than in lit review sections in an article or research paper)

2. **Body.**
   a) Summarize and synthesize: Give an overview of the main points of each source and combine them into a coherent whole.
   b) Analyze and interpret: Don't just paraphrase other researchers – add your own interpretations where possible, discussing the significance of findings in relation to the literature as a whole.
   c) Critically Evaluate: Mention the strengths and weaknesses of your sources.
   d) Write in well-structured paragraphs: Use transition words and topic sentence to draw connections, comparisons, and contrasts.

3. **Conclusion.**
   a) Summarize the key findings you have taken from the literature and emphasize their significance.
   b) Connect it back to your primary research question.

**Literature Review Strategies**

The following are brief descriptions of techniques that you might use in your literature review. Choose the approaches that are the most pertinent to your rhetorical situation.

1. **Summary.** Briefly state the argument and main points of relevant research.
2. **Synthesis.** Combine ideas in order to form an integrated theory or system through critical evaluation, compare/contrast, etc.
3. **Analysis**. Closely examine the elements or structure of the research and interpret through the lens of the field.
4. **Evaluation.** Assess the research based on criteria you choose, state, and explain. Support your evaluation with research.

## Illustrative Example of Literature Review

**Thesis Statement:** Service-learning programs implemented in American undergraduate universities since 2000 have not only proven beneficial for the individuals or organizations being served but also for the participating students by offering opportunities for academic, emotional, and social growth.

Prior studies have identified many benefits for educational institutions from service-learning programs. These benefits include positive perceptions of the university by the community (Miron & Moely, 2006), enhanced student retention rates (Eyler et al., 2001), positive teaching and learning outcomes such as greater student involvement and participation in class (Caruso et al., 2007), and increased opportunities for meaningful research and scholarly activities (Strand et al., 2003).

In this study and related research, the individuals serving are university students who are collaborating with the community partner. The studied benefits to individuals serving include cultural awareness sharing (Crabtree, 2008), as well as networking opportunities and application of classroom learning to real-world issues (Bowen et al., 2009). Ultimately, service-learning stimulates student learning and engages students in their surrounding communities. Service learning creates new goals for students such as personal development, career development, moral development, academic achievement, and "reflective civic participation" (Lamb et al., 1998). These types of projects allow students to utilize material learned in the classroom to improve societal conditions.

Integrating concepts and theories learned in the classroom with everyday life makes students more capable of highlighting the importance of each course. Additionally, material learned in business courses can be applied to benefit the community through a variety of tangible services, such as business planning or marketing new programs. Service learning is an excellent way for students to apply their course lessons to real-world situations

**Summary of key research**

**Evaluation and application to thesis/topic**

**Analysis and Synthesis**

## Conjunctions & Transitional Markers for In -text Citation

A. **In connecting concepts**

(Likewise, and, more so, moreover, also, in addition, more than, similarly, like, relatively, concomitant to, cognizant to, affirmatively, in juxtaposition, engagingly, connectedly, interconnectedly, in correlation, proportionally, relatively, similarly, congruently).

B. **In citing examples, elaboration and discussion.**

(Just like, on the same way (hand, end), to enumerate, listed down, just like, somewhat like, for example, to explain, to expound, elaborate, given the chance, to elaborate, to substantiate, accordingly, in details, comprehensively, tantamount to, in detail, in capsule, in a nutshell, accordingly, in retrospect, clearly, as per, deemed, subsequently, explicably)

C. **In contrast**

(However, on the hand, on the other end, but on the other side, compared with, unlike, in contradictory (contrast), paradoxically, opposite wise, on the other hand, on the contrary, reciprocally, oppositely).

D. **In synthesizing**

(therefore, thus, hence, henceforth, so that, so because, that is why, due to, caused by, thereby, as such, thereby, in summary, in conclusion, in effect, that is why, in turn, definitely, in general, as a whole, holistically, entirely, truly, constantly, logically, operationally, absolutely, apparently)

E. **In transitioning concepts and ideas**

(meanwhile, as such, in a way, consequently, taking aside, cognizantly, paramount to, concomitantly, in request for, in favor of, in quest for, looking forward to, behaviorally, emergently)

F. **In stressing a point or position on an issue.**

(Definitely, precisely, absolutely, entirely, irrevocably, soundly, strongly, perfectly, impeccably, intensively, concisely, ultimately, needlessly, seemingly, optimally, preferably, proportionally, as ground, as a result, as a matter of fact, in fact, subsequently, painstakingly, apparently, significantly, incessantly, presumably, legally, competitively, seriously, perfectly, intentionally, essentially, really, immeasurably, enticingly, unquestionably, emphatically, consistently, consistently, effectively, efficiently, enticingly, unconsciously, propositionally, probably, approximately, anticipatedly)

G. **In analyzing data**

(Interestingly, vehemently, amazingly, unbelievably, inevitably, intentionally, presumably, notably, remarkably, commendably, impartially, noticeably, sequentially, immeasurably, continuously, uninterruptedly, sustainably, seemingly, requisitely, instantly, impressively, accurately, tangibly, in accordance to, deemed, essential, necessarily, critically).

## Writing Proposed Innovation, Intervention and Strategy

Describe the action that you will do in order to solve your identified practical problem. A literature review would help you a lot in choosing and deciding on the intervention/strategy to use. Though action research is not conducted to fill the gap in the literature, adapting strategies from literature to solve a similar problem would be helpful. You may also discuss the issue with your co-teachers who experienced the same in his/her class. Sharing of thoughts, opinions and experiences would lead you to a better understanding of the problem.

Most action researches are reactive which means that the researches employ intervention in order to solve a problem. With the existing situation as the baseline, you decide on a solution (most of the time you believe will help address it. Some action researches are innovative which mean researcher would like to formulate his/her own strategy as an innovation and would test their effectiveness.

Nevertheless, regardless of the nature of the intervention, clearly describe the intervention or strategy that will be employed, who will be involved, and the activities that will be undertaken. Include also the rationale, extent, and limitation of the intervention, innovation or strategy. This part generally focuses on the "WHAT" of the action research.

## Illustrative Example of Proposed Innovation, Intervention and Strategy

### Effectiveness of Claim, Evidence, and Reasoning as an Innovation to Develop Students' Scientific Argumentative Writing Skills (Samosa, 2021)

### Proposed Innovation, Intervention and Strategy

In this action research, the researcher utilized the used CER framework by McNeil and Krajcik (2011), along with a CER template (appendix A), to help students formulate their explanations and arguments. The framework breaks down scientific arguments or explanations into three components. These components include a claim, evidence, and reasoning. The claim in a scientific explanation is the answer to a specific question or problem. Often times this claim is made after a scientific investigation that was performed in response to a prompt. The evidence component of the framework includes data that is collected through scientific investigation or data that is provided from previous research. This data can be quantitative or qualitative and is used to help support a claim that has been made. The reasoning component helps connect the evidence that you have cited to the claim that you have made. Based on previous experience with conclusion writing with students, the reasoning component tends to be the most difficult. Good reasoning often times includes connections to scientific concepts and principles that help students make better sense of data and trends.

These are process in utilization of the CER framework as follows.
Before direct instruction on the CER framework, students were administered a pre-intervention writing assessment. The purpose of the writing assessment was to assess students' current ability to formulate a scientific explanation. Because researcher was interested in the CER innovation effect on student use of scientific concepts in their reasoning, the writing assessment provided data related to a topic that was already covered in class. The writing assessment asked students to use a set of data related to bioenergetics to make a scientific explanation. This writing assessment was scored with a rubric that provided marks ranging from 1-4 for the claim, evidence, and reasoning (Appendix D). Students were also asked to take a pre- intervention survey (Appendix G). The pre-intervention survey served as a tool to gain insight into what students thought a scientific explanation or claim was, and how comfortable they were with writing their own.

Direct instruction of the CER framework followed the pre-intervention writing assessment and survey and coincided with our unit on plants, photosynthesis, and respiration. Direct instruction included the explanation of the three components of the CER framework as well as the importance of it in the field of science. This direct instruction began a classroom discussion that followed the question, "Is a hot dog a sandwich?" This discussion served as a tool to introduce the importance of having evidence or reasoning in your argument in a non-science related topic. After discussion with students, the researcher used a PowerPoint presentation to explain what a claim is, what evidence is, and what reasoning is. During this presentation, researcher made the connection between having these three components in a strong argument, and that these three components are also crucial to having strong scientific explanations.

Following direct instruction and the analysis activity, students conducted two scientific investigations in which they wrote scientific explanations using the CER framework (Appendix C). The CER template was developed to help students organize their explanations during the writing process. The first investigation involved cell respiration and asked students to the answer the question ***how cells carry out functions required for life?*** "This guided- inquiry investigation had students design and carry out their own experiment. Students were asked to write a scientific explanation that answered the lab question using the CER format. During this investigation, the researcher used the CER rubric (Appendix D) and helped guide students in their first use of it. After students finished their writing, they received formative feedback with the CER rubric. (Appendix E)

The second and third investigation involved photosynthesis and cellular respiration the question ***How photosynthetic organisms use light energy to combine carbon dioxide and water to form energy-rich compounds?"*** and "***How organisms obtain and utilize energy?".*** Students were asked to write a scientific explanation using the CER format. Use of the CER template was once again encouraged during the writing process. After drafting a conclusion, students were asked to analyze the explanations made by students from the other class

(Appendix C) and then grade the explanations using the CER rubric. Students then worked in small groups to share how they rated each explanation. A brief classroom discussion followed about the parts of the explanations that were done well and what parts needed improvement. Students then made final revisions to their writing before turning it in for formative feedback from the CER rubric.

Following the direct instruction and two investigations, students were administered the post-test writing assessment. This writing assessment was exactly the same as the pre-test writing assessment. Once again, the CER rubric was used to assess the claim, evidence, and reasoning in each explanation. Students were also given the post-intervention survey that was identical to the pre-intervention survey. Marks on the writing assessment and feedback from the survey was then analyzed and compared to the pre-intervention data.

Student interviews were also conducted with eight students (Appendix F). These interviews were done to help measure the effectiveness of the CER framework and template from the student perspective. The researcher was particularly interested in investigating whether or not the CER innovation helped students make connections to concepts from class more often than when the innovation is not implemented.

## Action Research Methods

Action Research Methods are the systematic tools used to recruit, sample, collect, analyze, and/or interpret information. Think of methods as the tools and techniques used for data collection and analysis. There are more methods than listed in the illustration (Samosa, 2021).

## Types of Research Methodologies

1. **Qualitative.** A methodology for exploring and understanding the meaning individuals or groups ascribe to a social or human problem. The question and procedures are emerging. It characterized by inductive analysis and flexibility.
2. **Quantitative.** A methodology for testing objective theories by examining the relationship among variables. Variables can be measured, typically on instruments, and numbered data can be analyzed using statistical procedures. Characterized by a structure and deductive data analysis. It aims at generalizability.
3. **Mixed research** combines quantitative and qualitative approaches by including both quantitative and qualitative data in a single study.

### Illustrative Example of Action Research Methods

**Effectiveness of Claim, Evidence, and Reasoning as an Innovation to Develop Students' Scientific Argumentative Writing Skills (Samosa, 2021)**

**Action Research Methods**

This study examines the instruction and implementation of a CER framework 63in 11th grade ABM students taking the subject Earth and Life Science in a qualitative and quantitative analysis. The motive behind this action research was to determine if the CER framework would improve students' ability to support claims in the science classroom through their own writing. More specifically, this study investigated how often students used data to support their claims, how often students used reasoning to link their evidence to their claim, and how often students used scientific principles or concepts when providing reasoning. This research was conducted on 11th grade ABM students taking the subject Earth and Life Science.

### Essential Elements of Research Methodology

1. **Research design.** It is a very important aspect of research methodology which describe the research mode (whether it is qualitative, quantitative, or mixed research, or if the researcher will use a specific research type e.g., descriptive, survey, historical, case or experimental).
2. **Respondent of the study.** This describes the target population and the sample frame.
3. **Instrument of the study.** It describes the specific type of research instrument that will be used such as questionnaire, checklist, questionnaire -checklist, interview, schedule, teacher -made-tests, and the like.
4. **Establishing and validating reliability.** The instrument must pass the validity and reliability test before it is utilized.
5. **Data Analysis**. One of the many ways of establishing the objectivity of research findings is by subjecting the data to different but appropriate data analysis and processes.

## Kinds of Qualitative Research Design

Qualitative research is a means for exploring and understanding the meaning individuals or groups ascribe to a social or human problem. The process of research involves emerging questions and procedures, data typically collected in the participant's setting, data analysis inductively building from particulars to general themes, and the researcher making interpretations of the meaning of the data. The final written report has a flexible structure. Those who engage in this form of inquiry support a way of looking at research that honors an inductive style, a focus on individual meaning, and the importance of rendering the complexity of a situation (adapted from Creswell, 2007).
These are the four common kinds of qualitative research design.

1. **Narrative** its collect stories from individuals (and documents, and group conversations) about individuals lived and told experiences. These stories may emerge from a story told to the researcher, a story that is co-constructed between the researcher and the participant, and a story intended as a performance to convey some message or point. Thus, there may be a strong collaborative feature of narrative research as the story emerges through the interaction or dialogue of the researcher and the participant(s).
2. **Phenomenology.** It describes the common meaning for several individuals of their lived experiences of a concept or a phenomenon. it focuses on describing what all participants have in common as they experience a phenomenon. The basic purpose of phenomenology is to reduce individual experiences with a phenomenon to a description of the universal essence (a "grasp of the very nature of the thing. The study of Dantay (2018) regarding the phenomenon of the Guidance-Teachers in the Philippines is an example of this.
3. **Grounded Theory.** intended is to move beyond description and to generate or discover a theory, a "unified theoretical explanation" for a process or an action. Participants in the study would all have experienced the process, and the development of the theory might help explain practice or provide a framework for further research. A key idea is that this theory development does not come "off the shelf" but rather is generated or "grounded" in data from participants who have experienced the process. Thus, grounded theory is a qualitative research design in which the inquirer generates a general explanation (a theory) of a process, an action, or an interaction shaped by the views of a large number of participants.
4. **Ethnography**. it focuses on an entire culture sharing group. It describes and interprets the shared and learned patterns of values, behaviors, beliefs, and language of a culture-sharing group. As a process,

ethnography involves extended observations of the group, most often through participant observation, in which the researcher is immersed in the day-to-day lives of the people and observes and interviews the group participants. Ethnographers study the meaning of the behavior, the language, and the interaction among members of the culture-sharing group.

## Kinds of Quantitative Research Design

Quantitative research is a means for testing objective theories by examining the relationship among variables. These variables, in turn, can be measured, typically on instruments, so that numbered data can be analyzed using statistical procedures. The final written report has a set structure consisting of introduction, literature and theory, methods, results, and discussion (Creswell, 2008). Like qualitative researchers, those who engage in this form of inquiry have assumptions about testing theories deductively, building in protections against bias, controlling for alternative explanations, and being able to generalize and replicate the findings.
There are four basic types of quantitative research, these are:

1. **Descriptive Research Design** - According to Ochave (1992), the principal aim of descriptive research is to describe the nature and the time of study and to explore the causes of phenomenon. It is also purposive process of gathering, analyzing, classifying and tabulating data about prevailing conditions, practices, belief, processes, trends cause – effect relationship and then make adequate and accurate interpretation about such data with or without the aid of **statistical** methods. It is concerned with the most appropriate methods to use to come up with adequate interpretation of the data and is purposive for accurate utilization of the significant variables that needs to emphasize the true meaning of the gathered data.

## Classification of Descriptive Research

a) **Descriptive - Correlational Research** – test for the relationship between two variables. Performing correctional research is done to establish what the effect of one on the other might be and how that affects the relationship. The purpose is to use two or more variables to better understand the condition of events that we encounter, to predict future conditions and events and correlation does not always mean causation. Another research study of Dantay (2022) focused on correlating the GAD program and services of Local Government

Units in Metro Manila is an example of this.

b) **Descriptive - Survey Research** - this research methods are employed to measure the existing phenomenon without inquiring into why it exists. In such studies, you do not consider the relationship between the variables. Your main intention is to use your data for problem solving rather than for hypothesis testing. Survey research have two scopes: census and sample. Census is a survey that covers the entire population of interest. Sample survey, on the other hand, is more which deals only with a portion of the population.

c) **Descriptive - Status Research** - this approach to problem - solving seeks to answer question to real facts relating to existing conditions. This is a technique of quantitative description which determines the prevailing conditions in a group of cases chosen for study. Several descriptive - status research stress current conditions with the assumption that things will change. They cover many traits or characteristics of the group.

d) **Descriptive - Analysis Research** - this method of research determines or describes the nature of an object by separating it into parts. Its purpose is to discover the nature of things. The researcher should determine the composition, structure. He also determines the individual parts and units integrated into an internal system. He should consider the forces that hold them together, and the strains that tend to destroy the system apart. He analyzes what makes the system work and regulates it.

e) **Descriptive - Classification Research -** this method is employed in natural sciences subjects, namely: Biology, Botany, Zoology, Phycology, Ichthyology, conchology, and like. The specimens collected, identified, and classified from taxonomic order.

f) **Descriptive - Evaluation Research** - this kind of research aims to assess the effects, impacts or outcomes of practices, policies, or program.

2. **Ex - Post Facto (Causal - Comparative) Research Design** - it looks to uncover a cause-and-effect relationship. This research is not conducted between the two groups on each other. They look solely for a statistically relationship between the two variable it tries to identify, specially, how the different groups are affected by the same circumstance. Causal - comparative research involves comparison. The study of two or more groups is done without focusing on their relations. The use of statistical is engaged to synthesize the data.

3. **Action Research Design** - this research follows a cyclical process. First, the researcher identifies a problem and determines a plan of action to

address it. Then, the action plan is implemented, and data is gathered to determine the effects of the action implemented. The information gathered during the implementation phase is analyzed and evaluated to gain a better understanding of the problem and determine the effectiveness of solution implemented. Action research is pragmatic and solution - driven, and any information gathered is used to identify and implement a solution to the problem. This design is appropriate for community - based situations. It requires the researcher to directly relate with his or her subjects and the community.

4. **Experimental Research Design** - This type of research seeks to determine the effect of one or more manipulative factors upon a dependent variable under controlled condition on a carefully controlled sample. The design compares the result obtained from an experimental sample with the control sample, which is practically identical to the experimental sample except for the one aspect whose effect is being tested. According to Ochave (1992) it also blueprints of the procedure that enables the researcher to test his hypothesis by reaching valid conclusions about relationships between independent and dependent variables and its conceptual framework within which the experiment is conducted

A. **Quasi - Experimental Research Design** - this type of design use to identify differences between two or more groups to explain causation. It allows researchers more control to make assumptions about causation and implication of findings. It is also useful when researchers want to study particular groups in which groups members cannot be randomly assigned. A major drawback to using quasi - experimental design is that these designs typically have less internal validity than do true experimental design.

**The following are some types of quasi - experimental design.**

a) **One - group posttest - only design** - type of experimental study in which only one group receives a treatment and is then measured in a posttest after treatment. In this design, there is no available comparison group or pretest data or baseline condition to compare with. This design is best implemented as an evaluation model.
b) **Static group comparison design** - this design attempt to make up for the lack of control groups but falls short in relation to showing if a change has occurred. In the static group comparison study, two groups are chosen, one of which receives the treatment and the other does not. A posttest score is then determined to measure the difference, after treatment, between the two groups. As you can see, this study does not include any

pre - testing and therefore any difference between the two groups prior to study are unknown.

c) **Nonequivalent control group design** - In nonequivalent control group design, a treatment group and a comparison group are compared using pretest and posttest measures. However, these groups are not randomly selected because they constitute naturally assembled groups. The assignment of X (the treatment) to one group or the other is randomly selected by the researcher.

d) **Time series design** - a quasi - experimental research design in which periodic measurements are made on a defined group of individuals both before and after implementation of an intervention. Time series studies are often conducted for the purpose of determining the intervention or treatment effect.

e) **Equivalent time - samples** - this design involves periodic introduction of treatment followed by measurement with the treatments varied consistently over time.

f) **Multiple time series design** - a type of quasi - experimental design where a series of periodic measurement is taken from two groups of test units (an experimental group and a control). The experimental group is exposed to a treatment and then another series of periodic measurements is taken from both groups.

g) **Equivalent material design** - this design involves giving equivalent samples of materials to subjects imparting interventions, and then making observation.

B. **True Experimental Research Design** - The true experimental research design control for nearly all sources of internal and external validity there is one obvious characteristics of these design and this is randomization. Also, there is the presence of a control group (Ochave, 1992).

According to Garcia (2003) Internal validity in experimental research refers to the basic minimum without which any experiment cannot be interpreted. The question a researcher must answer is whether the experimental treatment did make a difference in the experiment. On the other hand, External validity is the extent to which the results of an experimental can be generalized to people and environmental conditions outside the context of the experiment. It asks the question, how generalizable is the experiment? To what population, setting, treatment variables and measurement variables can be effect as noted in the experiment be generalized?

**Classification of True Experimental Research Design**

a) **Pretest - Posttest Control Group Design -** In this design, the experimental and control groups are carefully selected through appropriate randomization procedures. Each group is pre - tested on the dependent variable. Then the experimental condition or treatment is administered to the experimental group not to the control group, keeping all conditions the same for both groups. This is necessary so that the only difference is the manipulation of the independent variable. Each group is then post - tested on the dependent variable.

b) **Solomon Four Group Design -** This design is an extension of the pretest - posttest control group design and is used to eliminate the effect of pretest. It involves random assignment of subjects to four groups, with two groups being pretested and the two not. One of the pretested groups and one of the unpretested groups is subjected to experimental treatment. All the four groups, however, are post tested at the end of the experiment. Data are analyzed by doing an analysis of variance of the posttest scores.

c) **Posttest - only Control Group Design**- this design is the same as the pretest - posttest control group design, except that there are no pretests of the dependent variables.

C. **Pre - Experimental Research Design** - these are designs that do not possess two or more characteristics of experimental research.

1. **One - Shot Case Study** - In this design, the researcher administers a treatment and then makes an observation.
2. **One - Group Pretest - Posttest Design** - In this design, a single group of subjects is given a pretest, then the treatment and then test.
3. **Static Group Comparison** - In these two randomly selected groups are designed by chance, one to be the experimental group, the other the control group. The experimental group is exposed to variable X; the control group is not. At the close of the experiment, both groups are post tested, and a comparison is made between posttest result of each group to determine what has been the effect of the treatment.

**Kind of Mixed Research Design**

Mixed methods research is an approach to inquiry that combines or associates both qualitative and quantitative forms. It involves philosophical assumptions, the use of qualitative and quantitative approaches, and the mixing of both approaches in a study. Thus, it is more than simply collecting and analyzing both kinds of data; it also involves the use of both approaches in tandem so that

the overall strength of a study is greater than either qualitative or quantitative research (Creswell & Plano Clark, 2007).
There are four common kind of mixed methods design.

1. **Explanatory Sequential Mixed Design**. It is a design in mixed methods that appeals to individuals with a strong quantitative background or from fields relatively new to qualitative approaches. It involves a two-phase project in which the researcher collects quantitative data in the first phase, analyzes the results, and then uses the results to plan (or build on to) the second, qualitative phase. The quantitative results typically inform the types of participants to be purposefully selected for the qualitative phase and the types of questions that will be asked of the participants. The overall intent of this design is to have the qualitative data help explain in more detail the initial quantitative results. A typical procedure might involve collecting survey data in the first phase, analyzing the data, and then following up with qualitative interviews to help explain the survey responses.
2. **Exploratory Sequential Mixed design**. The reverse of the explanatory sequential approach and start with a qualitative phase first followed by a quantitative phase. Exploratory sequential mixed design is design in which the researcher first begins by exploring with qualitative data and analysis and then uses the findings in a second quantitative phase. Like the explanatory sequential approach, the second database builds on the results of the initial database. The intent of the strategy is to develop better measurements with specific samples of populations and to see if data from a few individuals (in qualitative phase) can be generalized to a large sample of a population (in quantitative phase). For example, the researcher would first collect focus group data, analyze the results, develop an instrument based on the results, and then administer it to a sample of a population. In this case, there may not be adequate instruments measuring the concepts with the sample that the investigator wishes to study. In effect, the researcher employs a three-phase procedure with the first phase as exploratory, the second as instrument development, and the third as administering the instrument to a sample of a population.
3. **Concurrent Triangulation Mixed Design**. In this design only one data collection phase is used, during which quantitative and qualitative data collection and analysis are conducted separately yet concurrently. The findings are integrated during the interpretation phase of the study. Usually, equal priority is given to both types of research.
4. **Concurrent Embedded Mixed Design**. In this design only one data collection phase is used, during which quantitative and qualitative data collection and analysis are conducted separately yet concurrently. The

findings are integrated during the interpretation phase of the study. Usually, equal priority is given to both types of research.

## Sample of Type of Research

**Effectiveness of Claim, Evidence, and Reasoning as an Innovation to Develop Students' Scientific Argumentative Writing Skills (Samosa, 2021)**

**Type of Research**

The researcher employed concurrent triangulation mixed design to evaluate the effectiveness of CER framework in developing student's scientific argumentation writing skills of selected of selected grade 11 Accountancy, Business and Management students at Graceville National High School – Senior High School Department. According to Fraenkel and Wallen (2010), it uses both quantitative and qualitative methods to study the same phenomenon in to determine if the two converge upon a single understanding of research problem investigated. In this design quantitative and qualitative methods are given equal priority, and all data are collected simultaneously.

## Sampling Design and Procedures

The basic unit for a survey is the population of the area in which it is performed. It is not usually possible to include the entire population so that people are selectively chosen to participate in a survey.

Sampling is the process of choosing a representative part of the population under study. "Typical" or representative of the population" means that a part of the population is chosen in such a manner that the characteristics and variation are reflected. It is, therefore, not just taking any part but rather that which is representative of the entire population (Sanchez, 1997).

The problem of sampling is one of the most important as well as one of the most difficult problems in social and behavioral science researchers. Orth (1976), a senior research scientist, point out that good sampling is an effective means of reducing the number of persons contacted to get a relatively accurate picture of the sample population's attitude and opinion.

A sample is a limited but representative subset of a population. It must however be adequate in size in order to be reliable. A good sample must be representative of the universe or population. A sample that is not representative of the population is known as biased sample. This may be due to imperfect instruments, the personal qualities of the observer, defective technique, or other causes (Yule & Kendall, 1990).

The term "population" is not necessarily synonymous with a population of people. A statistical population or universe may consist of attributes, qualities or behavior of people, the behavior of inanimate objects such as dice or coins, cities or city block, households or dwelling structures, the day's output of a factory, or opinions of the electorate of an entire nation.

There are two groups of population: the target population and the accessible population. The target population is composed of the entire group of people or objects to which the researcher wishes to generalize the findings of the study, while the accessible population is a portion of the population to which the researcher has reasonable access. For example, in a study about common difficulties encountered by senior high school students in their first semester of school year 2017-2018, the target population may be all senior high school students in metro manila. However, the researcher may have access only to the students of a specific school - these students comprise the accessible population.

Researchers commonly select samples for study rather than entire populations due to constraints in budget, time, and manpower. A good sample should be representative of the population, such that the characteristics of the population - especially those pertinent to the study - are reflected in the sample with a fair amount of accuracy.

The individual participants in the study are often referred to as subject or respondents. The subjects are individuals or entities which serve as the focus of the study. Respondents are individuals or groups of people who actively serve as source of information during data collection. The subjects of the study may also be its respondents, but there also times that these are two groups of different individuals or entities. Subject and respondents may also be referred to as elements - particularly if said elements are objects, rather than people.

Take for example a study focused on the behavior of the students who belong to broken families. The students who belong to these families are the subjects of the study, which may also be the respondents the researcher seeks to interview directly. If the researcher interviews or surveys the classmates of these students, the students remain the subjects and the classmate then become the respondents.

A statistic is a number describing a property of a sample, whereas a parameter is a number describing a property of a population. A statistic can be used to estimate the parameter in what is called a statistical inference. For example: a researcher, examining all marriages in the Philippines in the year 2016, wants to find a parameter - the mean age of all men in those marriages. From sample of 1,000 subjects, she obtains mean of 31 years. This figure is a statistic. Using this figure, she concludes that the mean age of Filipino men who married in 2016 is likely to be close to 31, as well.

It is important for the researcher to us an acceptable sample size to ensure that their study will be accurate. Generally, the larger the sample, the, more reliable the result of the study will be. Hence, it is advisable to have a sample large enough to yield reliable results, yet small enough to be manageable within the constraints of the study.

## Advantages of Sampling

The advantages of sampling are as follows:

1. **It saves time, money, and effort.** The researcher can save time, money, and effort because the number of subjects involved is small. With only a small number of subjects to be collected, tabulated, presented, analyzed and interpreted, the use of sample gives comprehensive information of the results of the study.
2. **It is more effective.** Sampling is more effective if every individual of the population without bias has an equal chance of being included in the sample and data are scientifically collected, analyzed, and interpreted.
3. **It is faster, cheaper and economical.** Since sample is only "drop in a bucket," the collection, tabulation, presentation, analysis and interpretation of data are rapid and less expensive due to small number of subjects and few copies of the questionnaires are used.
4. **It is more accurate.** Fewer errors are made due to small size of data involved n collection, tabulation, presentation, analysis and interpretation.
5. **It gives more comprehensive information.** Since there is a thorough investigation of the study due to small sample, the results give more comprehensive information because all members of the population have an equal chance of being included in the sample.

## Disadvantage of Sampling

If sampling design has strength, it also has its weakness. The disadvanta ges of sampling are as follows.

1. Sample data involve more care in preparing detailed subclassification due to small to small number of subjects.
2. If the sampling plan is not correctly designed and followed, the results may be misleading.
3. Sampling requires an expert to conduct the study in an area. If this is lacking, the result can be erroneous.

4. The characteristics to be observed may occur rarely in a population, for instance over 30 years of teaching experience o teachers with outstanding performance.
5. Complicated sampling plans are laborious to prepare.

**Factors to consider in determining the sample size. (Macmillian & Schumacher, 1989)**

1. Homogeneity of the population.
2. Degree of precision desired by the researcher.
3. Types of sampling procedure.
4. The Types of research
5. Research hypothesis
6. Financial constraints
7. Importance of the results
8. Numbers of variables studied.
9. Methods of data collection

**Various approaches to determining the Sample size.**

1. Sample sizes as small as 30 are generally adequate to ensure that the sampling distribution of the mean will approximate the normal curve (Shott, 1990).
2. When the total population is equal to or less than, this same number may serve as the sample size. This called universal sampling.
3. Slovin's formula is used to compute for sample size (Sevilla, 1990).

$$n = \frac{N}{1+Ne^2}$$

Where ***n*** stand for a sample; ***N***, the population size, and **e** is for desired margin of error

Example: the population total is 8,000 with a desired 2% margin of error

Given: **N** = 8,000; **e** = 0.02

$$n = \frac{N}{1+Ne^2}$$

$$= \frac{8,000}{1+8,000\,(0.02)^2}$$

$$= \frac{8,000}{1+8,000\,(0.0004)}$$

$$= \frac{8,000}{1+3.2}$$

$$= \frac{8,000}{4.2}$$

$$= 1,905$$

4. Minimum Sample Size Recommendations for Most Common Quantitative and Qualitative Research Designs by experts.

| Research Design | Minimum Sample Size Suggestion |
|---|---|
| **1. Correlational** | 64 participants for one-tailed hypotheses; 82 participants for two-tailed hypotheses (Onwuegbuzie et al., 2004) |
| **2. Causal-Comparative** | 51 participants per group for one-tailed hypotheses; 64 participants for two-tailed hypotheses (Onwuegbuzie et al., 2004) |
| **3. Experimental** | 21 participants per group for one-tailed hypotheses (Onwuegbuzie et al., 2004) |
| **4. Case Study** | 3-5 participants (Creswell, 2002) |
| **5. Phenomenological** | ≤ 10 interviews (Creswell, 1998);∃ ≥ 6 (Morse, 1994) |
| **6. Grounded Theory** | 15-20 (Creswell, 2002); 20-30 (Creswell, 2007) |
| **7. Ethnography** | 1 cultural group (Creswell, 2002); 30-50 interviews (Morse, 1994) |
| **8. Ethological** | 100-200 units of observation (Morse, 1994) |

| Sampling Design | Minimum Sample Size Suggestion |
|---|---|
| **1. Subgroup Sampling Design** | ≥ 3 participants per subgroup (Onwuegbuzie & Leech, 2007c) |
| **2. Nested Sampling Design** | ≥ 3 participants per subgroup (Onwuegbuzie & Leech, 2007c) |

| Data Collection Procedure | Minimum Sample Size Suggestion |
|---|---|
| **1. Interview** | 12 participants (Guest, Bunce, & Johnson, 2006) |
| **2. Focus Group** | 6-9 participants (Krueger, 2000); 6-10 participants (Langford, Schoenfeld, & Izzo, 2002; Morgan, 1997); 6-12 participants (Johnson & Christensen, 2004); 6-12 participants (Bernard, 1995); 8–12 participants (Baumgartner, Strong, & Hensley, 2002). 3 to 6 focus groups (Krueger, 1994; Morgan, 1997; Onwuegbuzie, Dickinson, Leech, & Zoran, 2007) |

For correlational, causal-comparative, and experimental research designs, the recommended sample sizes represent those needed to detect a medium (using Cohen's [1988] criteria), one-tailed statistically significant relationship or difference with .80 power at the 5% level of significance.

5. To estimate a proportion in a population:

$$\textbf{Sample size} = [\,(\text{z-score})^2 \times p(1-p)\,] \div (\text{margin of error})^2$$

The margin of error is what you are prepared to accept (usually between 1% and 10%);

The z-score, also called the z value, is found from statistical tables, and depends on the confidence interval chosen (90%, 95% and 99% are commonly used, so choose which one you want);

p is your estimate of what the proportion is likely to be. You can often estimate p from previous research, but if you cannot do that then use 0.5.

6. To estimate a population, mean:

   **Margin of error = t × (s ÷ square root of the sample size).**

   Margin of error is what you are prepared to accept (usually between 1% and 10%)

   If the sample size is larger than about 30, t is equivalent to the z score, and available from statistical tables as before;

   s is the standard deviation, which is usually guessed, based on previous experience or another research.

7. By using the Calmorin's formula, the problem is solved as follows.

$$S_s = \frac{NV+[\,Se^2\ (1-p)]}{NSe+\ [V^2\ \ p\ (1-p)]}$$

Where $S_s$ stand for sample size; $N$, the population; $V$ standard value (2.58) of 1 percent level of probability with 0.99 reliability level; $Se$, sampling error (0.01); and $p$, the largest possible proportion (0.50).
Example: Getting from a parameter of 900.
Given: **N** = 900; **V** = 2.58; **Se** = 0.01; **p** = 0.50

$$S_s = \frac{NV+[\,Se^2\ (1-p)]}{NSe+\ [V^2\ \ p\ (1-p)]}$$

$$= \frac{900(2.58)+[\,(0.01)^2\ (1-0.50)]}{900(0.01)+\ [(2.58)^2\ \ (0.50)(1-0.50)]}$$

$$= \frac{2322+\ (0.0001)\ (0.50)}{9+\ (6.6564)(0.50)(0.50)}$$

$$= \frac{2322+\ 0.00005}{9+\ 6.6564(0.25)}$$

$$= \frac{2322+\ 0.00005}{9+\ 1.6641} = \mathbf{218}$$

**Steps in sample design**

While developing a sampling design, the researcher must pay attention to the following points:

1. **Type of universe:** The first step in developing any sample design is to clearly define the set of objects, technically called the Universe, to be studied. The universe can be finite or infinite. In finite universe the number of items is certain, but in case of an infinite universe the number of items is infinite, i.e., we cannot have any idea about the total number of items. The

population of a city, the number of workers in a factory and the like are examples of finite universes, whereas the number of stars in the sky, listeners of a specific radio programme, throwing of a dice etc. are examples of infinite universes.

2. **Sampling unit:** A decision has to be taken concerning a sampling unit before selecting sample. Sampling unit may be a geographical one such as state, district, village, etc., or a construction unit such as house, flat, etc., or it may be a social unit such as family, club, school, etc., or it may be an individual. The researcher will have to decide one or more of such units that he has to select for his study.
3. **Source list:** It is also known as 'sampling frame' from which sample is to be drawn. It contains the names of all items of a universe (in case of finite universe only). If source list is not available, researcher has to prepare it. Such a list should be comprehensive, correct, reliable and appropriate. It is extremely important for the source list to be as representative of the population as possible.
4. **Size of sample:** This refers to the number of items to be selected from the universe to constitute a sample. This major problem before a researcher. The size of sample should neither be excessively large, nor too small. It should be optimum. An optimum sample is one which fulfills the requirements of efficiency, representativeness, reliability, and flexibility. While deciding the size of sample, researcher must determine the desired precision as also an acceptable confidence level for the estimate. The size of population variance needs to be considered as in case of larger variance usually a bigger sample is needed. The size of population must be kept in view for this also limits the sample size. The parameters of interest in a research study must be kept in view, while deciding the size of the sample. Costs too dictate the size of sample that we can draw. As such, budgetary constraint must invariably be taken into consideration when we decide the sample size.
5. **Parameters of interest:** In determining the sample design, one must consider the question of the specific population parameters which are of interest. For instance, we may be interested in estimating the proportion of persons with some characteristic in the population, or we may be interested in knowing some average or the other measure concerning the population. There may also be important sub-groups in the population about whom we would like to make estimates. All this has a strong impact upon the sample design we would accept.
6. **Budgetary constraint:** Cost considerations, from practical point of view, have a major impact upon decisions relating to not only the size of the sample but also to the type of sample. This fact can even lead to the use of a non-probability sample.

7. **Sampling procedure:** Finally, the researcher must decide the type of sample he will use i.e., he must decide about the technique to be used in selecting the items for the sample. In fact, this technique or procedure stands for the sample design itself. There are several sample designs (explained in the pages that follow) out of which the researcher must choose one for his study. Obviously, he must select that design which, for a given sample size and for a given cost, has a smaller sampling error.

**Criteria of Selecting a Sampling Procedure**

In this context one must remember that two costs are involved in a sampling analysis viz., the cost of collecting the data and the cost of an incorrect inference resulting from the data. Researcher must keep in view the two causes of incorrect inferences viz., systematic bias and sampling error. Systematic bias results from errors in the sampling procedures, and it cannot be reduced or eliminated by increasing the sample size. At best the causes responsible for these errors can be detected and corrected. Usually, a systematic bias is the result of one or more of the following factors:

1. **Inappropriate sampling frame:** If the sampling frame is inappropriate i.e., a biased representation of the universe, it will result in a systematic bias.
2. **Defective measuring device:** If the measuring device is constantly in error, it will result in systematic bias. In survey work, systematic bias can result if the questionnaire or the interviewer is biased. Similarly, if the physical measuring device is defective there will be systematic bias in the data collected through such a measuring device.
3. **Non-respondents:** If we are unable to sample all the individuals initially included in the sample, there may arise a systematic bias. The reason is that in such a situation the likelihood of establishing contact or receiving a response from an individual is often correlated with the measure of what is to be estimated.
4. **Indeterminacy principle:** Sometimes we find that individuals act differently when kept under observation than what they do when kept in non-observed situations. For instance, if workers are aware that somebody is observing them in course of a work study based on which the average length of time to complete a task will be determined and accordingly the quota will be set for piece work, they generally tend to work slowly in comparison to the speed with which they work if kept unobserved. Thus, the indeterminacy principle may also be a cause of a systematic bias.
5. **Natural bias in the reporting of data:** Natural bias of respondents in the reporting of data is often the cause of a systematic bias in many inquiries. There is usually a downward bias in the income data collected by government taxation department, whereas we find an upward bias in the income data collected by some social organization. People in general

understate their incomes if asked about it for tax purposes, but they overstate the same if asked for social status or their affluence. Generally, in psychological surveys, people tend to give what they think is the 'correct' answer rather than revealing their true feelings.

*Sampling errors* are the random variations in the sample estimates around the true population parameters. Since they occur randomly and are equally likely to be in either direction, their nature happens to be of compensatory type and the expected value of such errors happens to be equal to zero. Sampling error decreases with the increase in the size of the sample, and it happens to be of a smaller magnitude in case of homogeneous population.

*Sampling error* can be measured for a given sample design and size. The measurement of sampling error is usually called the 'precision of the sampling plan'. If we increase the sample size, the precision can be improved. But increasing the size of the sample has its own limitations viz., a large sized sample increases the cost of collecting data and enhances the systematic bias. Thus, the effective way to increase precision is usually to select a better sampling design which has a smaller sampling error for a given sample size at a given cost. In practice, however, people prefer a less precise design because it is easier to adopt the same and also because of the fact that systematic bias can be controlled in a better way in such a design.

In brief, *while selecting a sampling procedure, researcher must ensure that the procedure causes a relatively small sampling error and helps to control the systematic bias in a better way.*

## Characteristics of a good sample design

From what has been stated above, we can list down the characteristics of a good sample design as under:

a) Sample design must result in a truly representative sample.
b) Sample design must be such which results in a small sampling error.
c) Sample design must be viable in the context of funds available for the research study.
d) Sample design must be such so that systematic bias can be controlled in a better way.
e) Sample should be such that the results of the sample study can be applied, in general, for the universe with a reasonable level of confidence.

## Sampling in Qualitative Research

Qualitative researchers typically make sampling choices that enable them to deepen understanding of whatever phenomenon it is that they are studying. Qualitative researchers typically employ when sampling as well as the various types of samples that qualitative researchers are most likely to use in their work.

Non-probability sampling represents a group of sampling techniques that help researchers to select units from a population that they are interested in studying. Collectively, these units form the sample that the researcher studies. A core characteristic of non-probability sampling techniques is that samples are selected based on the subjective judgement of the researcher, rather than random selection (i.e., probabilistic methods), which is the cornerstone of probability sampling techniques.

| Nonprobability Sampling Design | Descriptions |
|---|---|
| 1. Purposive | Researcher seeks out elements that meet specific criteria. |
| 2. Snowball | Researcher relies on participant referrals to recruit new participants. |
| 3. Quota | Researcher selects cases from within several different subgroups. |
| 4. Convenience | Researcher gathers data from whatever cases happen to be convenient |

**Sampling in Quantitative Research**

Quantitative researchers are often interested in being able to make generalizations about groups larger than their study samples. While there are certainly instances when quantitative researchers rely on nonprobability samples (e.g., when doing exploratory or evaluation research), quantitative researchers tend to rely on probability sampling techniques. The goals and techniques associated with probability samples differ from those of nonprobability samples.

Unlike nonprobability sampling, **probability sampling** refers to sampling techniques for which a person's (or event's) likelihood of being selected for membership in the sample is known. You might ask yourself why we should care about a study element's likelihood of being selected for membership in a researcher's sample. The reason is that, in most cases, researchers who use probability sampling techniques are aiming to identify a representative sample from which to collect data. A representative sample is one that resembles the population from which it was drawn in all

the ways that are important for the research being conducted. If, for example, you wish to be able to say something about differences between men and women at the end of your study, you better make sure that your sample does not contain only women. That is a bit of an oversimplification, but the point with representativeness is that if your population varies in some way that is important to your study, your sample should contain the same sorts of variation.

Obtaining a representative sample is important in probability sampling because a key goal of studies that rely on probability samples is generalizability. In fact, generalizability is perhaps the key feature that distinguishes probability samples from nonprobability samples. **Generalizability** refers to the idea that a study's results will tell us something about a group larger than the sample from which the findings were generated. In order to achieve generalizability, a core principle of probability sampling is that all elements in the researcher's target population have an equal chance of being selected for inclusion in the study.

In research, this is the principle of **random selection**. Random selection is a mathematical process that we will not go into too much depth about here, but if you have taken or plan to take a statistics course, you will learn more about it there. The important thing to remember about random selection here is that, as previously noted, it is a core principal of probability sampling. If a researcher uses random selection techniques to draw a sample, he or she will be able to estimate how closely the sample represents the larger population from which it was drawn by estimating the sampling error. Sampling error is a statistical calculation of the difference between results from a sample and the actual parameters of a population.

## Types of Probability Samples

There are a variety of probability samples that researchers may use. These include the following.

| Probability Sampling Design | Descriptions |
|---|---|
| **1. Simple random** | Researcher randomly selects elements from sampling frame |
| **2. Systematic** | Researcher selects every *k*th element from sampling frame. |
| **3. Stratified** | Researcher creates subgroups then randomly selects elements from each subgroup. |
| **4. Cluster** | Researcher randomly selects clusters then randomly selects elements from selected clusters. |

## Illustrative Example of Sample and Sampling Techniques

**Cooperative Learning Approach as Innovation to Improve Students' Academic Achievement and Attitude in Teaching Biology (Samosa, 2020)**

**Sample and Sampling Techniques**

The subjects of the experiment were 30 students from the two intact section of Grade 11 student from the Towerville National High School., a Public School in Division of City of San Jose del Monte Bulacan this A.Y. 2018-2019. The students were purposively selected according to their strand TechVoc (Home Economics) and TechVoc (ICT). Two sections were selected to be the participants of the experiment based on their previous grades in earth and life science.

**Table 1: Frequency and Percentage of the Respondents during the Research Study.**

| Group | Frequency | Percentage |
|---|---|---|
| **Control Group (TVL: ICT)** | 15 | 50% |
| **Experimental Group (TVL: HE)** | 15 | 50% |
| **TOTAL** | 30 | 100% |

## Research Instruments

Research Instrument it is a tool used to collect, measure, and analyze data related to research interests and is tied to the research methodology.
Research Instruments may be any of the following:

1. **Researcher- made instrument** is instrument/test constructed by researcher and is not carefully prepared as standardized instrument/test.
2. **Adopting an instrument** is quite simple and requires very little effort. Even when an instrument is adopted, though, there still might be a few modifications that are necessary.
3. **Adapting an instrument** requires more substantial changes than adopting an instrument. In this situation, the researcher follows the general design of another instrument but adds items, removes items, and/or substantially changes the content of each item.

   Whenever possible, it is best for an instrument to be adopted. When this is not possible, the next best option is to adapt an instrument. However, if there are no other instruments available, then the last option is to develop an instrument.

## Characteristics of Research Instruments

1. **Reliability** - is the consistency of your measurement, or the degree to which an instrument measures the same way each time it is used under the same condition with the same subjects. In short, it is the repeatability of your measurement. A measure is considered reliable if a person's score on the same test given twice is similar. It is important to remember that reliability is not measured, it is estimated. A good instrument will produce consistent scores. An instrument's reliability is estimated using a correlation coefficient of one type or another.
2. **Validity** is the extent to which a test measures what it claims to measure. It

is vital for a test to be valid in order for the results to be accurately applied and interpreted. Validity isn't determined by a single statistic, but by a body of research that demonstrates the relationship between the test and the behavior it is intended to measure. There are three types of validity: It is the strength of our conclusions, inferences or propositions. More formally, Cook and Campbell (1979) define it as the "best available approximation to the truth or falsity of a given inference, proposition or conclusion. "

3. **Practicability** - It should be feasible & usable. Quality of being usable in context to the objective to be achieved.
4. **Measurability** - It should measure the objective to be achieved.

**Séquence for Questionnaire/Instrument/test Development.**

**STEP 1 : Content Validity.** This is considered the most crucial procedure in the test construction process because content validity sets the pace for the succeedings validity and reliability measures. Content Validity is the degree to which the test represents the essence, the topics, and the areas that test is designed to measure. The test items need to be a representative sample of the content of the variable being measured. Content Validity is generally reported in terms of non-numeral data unlike the other types of Validity. But it is the primary concern of the test developer because it is the content of the items that really reflects the 'whatness' of the property intended to be measured.

The following procedure and techniques are suggested to achieve a high degree of content validity.

1. **Documentary analysis or pre-survey.** You may start from where you temporarily ended your review of the literature. At this stage, you must have familiarized yourself with the theoretical construct directly related to the test you are planning. The literature you reviewed must have provided you a comprehensive knowledge of the nature of the test criterion. If you have not done this, you may have to review some more related studies relevant to your own undertaking. Focus your related studies relevant to your own undertaking. Focus your attention to the tests used, purposes of the said tests, the areas covered, format, scaling techniques, etc.
2. **Development of a Table of Specification (TOS).** Determining the areas or concepts that will represent the nature of the variable being measured and the relative emphasis of each area are essentially judgmental. It takes a broad knowledge of the subject matter to be able to make a good judgement. Assuming that you are prepared for this, you are now ready to lay out a Table of Specification (TOS). A detailed TOS includes areas or concepts, objectives, number of items, and percentage or proportion of items in each area. It advisable to make a 50 to 100 percent allowance in the construction of items. This means that if you intend to have 100 items for the final draft, you should start the initial draft with 150 to 200 items. In way, enough allowance is

provided for items that might be discarded by the validation procedures.

3. **Consultation with Expert.** Let us say that now you have employed judgements in representing the population of areas or concepts that make up the variable you intend to measure. However, your judgment is limited to your competence. At this point it is advisable to consult with your thesis advisers or with some authorities who are expertise in making judgement about the representativeness or relevance of the entries made in your TOS.
4. **Item Writing.** As soon as you have finalized your TOS incorporating valuable suggestions by the experts you have consulted, you can begin writing the items for each of the areas in the TOS. At this stage you should know type of items you are supposed to construct: the type of instrument, format, scaling and scoring techniques. Obviously, you also need to be familiar with possibilities and limitations of the varieties of test items. You are supposed to have gotten ideas from your review of related literature. Constructing good items is not an easy task. These are materials that may provide useful pointers for item writing, but there are not hard and straightforward rules that guarantee production of good items. Every test item is based on your creative talent as the item writer and your background about the test content. While the TOS presents the areas to be covered by the test, it does not really specify the content and purposes of each individual item. The quality of the test items, therefore, depends to a consideration extent upon your ability to produce ideas and translate them into items that satisfy the TOS.

**STEP 2: Face Validation.** Face validity, the crudest type of validity, pertains to whether the test looks like it can measure what you intend to measure. The test items are ocularly inspected and later on judged superficially if they are valid enough to measure the variable being measured. However, an instrument that presents only its face validity, more often than not, is an open target for criticism. This is because generally, this type of validity is not supported by any evidence that the test really measures anything. Without content validation, this type of validity cannot stand alone for use especially in researches at the graduate level. There are ways, however, by which we can reinforce the face validity of an instrument.

1. **Item Inspection**. Have the initial draft of the instrument inspected by a group of evaluators such as thesis adviser, test construction experts, teachers/professionals whose specialization are related to the subject matter at hand. Be sure to give the evaluators a set of criteria on which to base their judgment (appropriateness or suitability of items, relevance, clarity of language used, correctness of sentences, etc.) Very often, for achievement tests and other educational tests. The evaluators can also inspect obviously right/wrong. Half-true or misleading distractors. Sometimes the evaluators make the necessary corrections right on the draft given to them. The table below can serve as summary of evaluation made by the aforementioned people.
2. 

**Item Inspection.**

| Item No. | Suitable | Not Suitable | Need Revision |
|---|---|---|---|
| | | | |
| | | | |

To expedite evaluation, the last three columns above can place beside the items right on the draft of the test. The headings should be defined by the test developer. For instance, suitability of items may mean that the items is valid in terms of its content, language level and relevance. Not suitable would mean otherwise. It is also possible that the evaluator may check the first and last columns for the same item. This would mean that the item is valid content- wise but needs some technical revisions, e.g. is grammar, choice of words, attractiveness of distractors, etc.

3. **Inter – judge Consistency**. You may collate the data gathered from the evaluators for analysis. If you have requested three persons, for instance, to inspect your first draft, you will have to look at the agreement or consistency of judgement they made about each of the items. If an item is judges by at least two out of the three evaluators as a suitable item then the item can be retained. Loo at the notes or comments made by the evaluators and judge the merit of their suggestions. There may be items which are strongly suggested for revision. For items consistently judged as unsuitable, these are supposed to be discarded from the second draft. Before ending this step, you might want to check the proportions of the items in the TOS. Find out if after culling the poor items, the proportion for each area has not been grossly affected if very few items are left, you may have to revise the poor items.

**STEP 3: Fist Trial Run.** At this stage, must have already stenciled your first draft as a result of Step 1 and 2, now you are ready for the first try -out. Be sure to try out your test or a sample that is comparable to your target population or final example. The try -out sample should be enough to provide meaningful computations. There are two purposes of the first trial run. One is to determine the language suitability of the items and ease in following directions from the point of view of the examinees. The average length of time to finish the test and other problems relevant to taking the test are also determined. Second, the trial run is for judging good and poor items quantitatively. The latter pertains to item analysis. This process determines internal consistency, or item homogeneity and the discriminability and difficulty of the items.

**STEP 4: Item Analysis.** Both the validity and reliability of any test depend largely on the characteristics of items. Consequently, high validity and reliability can be built into the instruments in advance through item analysis. This process checks whether each item is "differentiating". Likert (1967) explains that by undifferentiating, it means that the statement does not measure what the battery of items measures and hence to include it contributes nothing to be scale. In attitude testing, for instance, Likert further states that "item analysis can be used as an objective check to determine whether the members of a group react differentially to the battery, that is, item analysis indicates whether those persons who fall towards one end of the attitude continuum of the battery do so the particular statement, and vice versa." Thus, item analysis reveals the satisfactoriness of any statement as far as its inclusion in a given attitude scale is concerned.

**The following are purposes of item analysis**.

a) to select the best available items for the final form of the test;
b) to identify structural or content defects in the items;
c) to detect learning difficulties of the classes as a whole; and
d) to identify the areas of weakness of students in need of remediation or innovation.

**There are three main elements in an item analysis. These elements are as follows:**

1. examination of the difficulty level of the items;
2. determinations of the discriminating power of each item, and
3. examination of the effectiveness of the distractors in a multiple-choice item.

The difficulty level of an item is known as ***index of difficulty***. By the index of difficulty is meant the percentage of students answering correct each item in the test. On the other hand, ***index of discrimination*** refers to the percentage of high scoring individuals responding correctly to an item. This numeral index indicates how effectively an item differentiates between the students who did well and those who did poorly on the test.

**METHOD 1: The U-L Index Method**. This technique was advanced by John Stocklein (1957) and is appropriate for test whose criterion is measured along a continuous scale (e.g. scholastic ratings, job ratings, performance records, achievement test scores) and whose individual item is scored right or wrong and positive or negative. The technique employs the following steps.

a) Arrange test scores from highest to lowest. This ranking is based on the student's total score on the test.
b) Get one – third of the papers from the highest scores and other third from the lowest scores. These two extreme sets of examination papers are the criterion groups. The first is the upper group and the latter is the lower group. The middle group is not used in the analysis of test items.
c) Record separately the number of times each alternative was chosen by the students in both groups.
d) Add the number of correct answers to each item made by the combined upper and lower groups.
e) Compute the index of difficulty for each item, following the formula:

$$\textbf{IDF} = \left(\frac{\text{NRC}}{\text{TS}}\right) 100$$

Where : **IDF** = index of difficulty
**NRC** = number of students responding correctly to an item,
**TS** = total number of students in the upper and lower groups.

f) Compute the index of discrimination, based on the formula

$$\textbf{IDN} = \left(\frac{\text{CU}-\text{CL}}{\text{NSG}}\right)$$

Where : IDN = index of discrimination
CU = number of correct responses of the upper group
CL= number of correct responses of the lower groups.
NSG = number of students per group

Sample item data and resulting indices derived from the procedures described in this discussion are presented below.

| Item | Group | Answer | | | | Total No. Correct answer | Difficulty Index | Difficulty Level | H-L | Discrimination Index | Verbal Description |
|---|---|---|---|---|---|---|---|---|---|---|---|
| | | A | B | C | D | | | | | | |
| 1 | H – 20 | 3 | ***14*** | 2 | 1 | | | | | | |
| | L – 20 | 10 | 7 | 3 | 0 | 21 | 52.5 | Average | 7 | 0.35 | Good item |
| 2 | H – 20 | 0 | 0 | ***18*** | 2 | | | | | | |
| | L – 20 | 0 | 3 | ***9*** | 8 | 27 | 67.5 | Easy | 9 | 0.45 | Very Good item |
| 3 | H – 20 | 4 | ***8*** | 4 | 4 | | | | | | |
| | L – 20 | 10 | ***2*** | 4 | 4 | 10 | 25.0 | Difficult | 6 | 0.30 | Good item |
| 4 | H – 20 | 3 | 3 | 4 | ***10*** | | | | | | |
| | L – 20 | 2 | 4 | 10 | ***4*** | 14 | 35.0 | Difficult | 6 | 0.30 | Good item |
| 5 | H – 20 | ***15*** | 2 | 2 | 1 | | | | | | |
| | L – 20 | ***1*** | 10 | 4 | 5 | 16 | 40.0 | Difficult | 14 | 0.70 | Very Good item |

*italicized number indicate correct answers.
* number of students tested = 60

The difficulty index of a test is important because it tells a teacher something meaningful about the comprehension of or performance on, material or task contained in an item. A closer look at the sample item data presented above reveals that items 2 is easy as its difficulty index is 67.5%. the same is true with item 1, with an estimated difficulty index of 52.5%.

The foregoing points to one thing – the higher the value of the difficulty index, the easier is the item. This is because difficulty index represents the percentage of the total number of students answering an item correctly. Thus, there is an inverse relationship between the magnitude of the index and what it purports to represent. For an item to be considered a good item, its difficulty index should be 50%. An item with 50% difficulty index is neither is 67.5% easy and 32.5% difficult. Information on the index of difficulty of an item can help a researcher/teacher decide whether a test item should be revised, retained, or modified.

Difficulty index of a test item can be interpreted with the use of the table of equivalents:

| Range | Difficulty Level |
|---|---|
| 20 & below | Very Difficult |
| 21- 40 | Difficult |
| 41- 60 | Average |
| 61 – 80 | Easy |
| 81 & above | Very Easy |

On the other hand, the index of discrimination, as already pointed out, tells a researcher/teacher the degree to which a test item differentiates the higher achievers from the low achievers in his/her class or test administration. With regard to item construction, a test item may have positive or negative discriminating power.

An item has a positive discriminating power when more students from the upper group got the right answer than those from the lower group. Conversely, when more students from the lower group, the item has a negative discriminating power. These are, however, instances when an item has a zero-discriminating power. This happens when there is an equal number of students/participants from both the upper and lower groups who got the right answer to a test item.

From the sample item data earlier presented, it can be noted that item 5 has the highest discrimination power as its calculated index of discrimination of 0.70. This means that items 5 can differentiate high and low achievers.

Index of discrimination of the test item can be interpreted with the use of the table of equivalents

| Range | Difficulty Level |
|---|---|
| .40 & above | Very Good Item |
| .30 - .39 | Good Item |
| .20 - .29 | Fair Item |
| .09 - .19 | Poor Item |

The question at this point is when should a test item be rejected? retained? modified or revised? a test item can be retained when its level of difficulty is average and discriminating power is positive. It has to be rejected when it is either easy/very easy or difficult and its discriminating power is negative or zero. On the other hand, an item can be modified when it difficulty level is average and its discrimination index is negative.

An ideal item is one that all students/participants in the upper group answer correctly the lower group have to be evenly distributed among the incorrect alternatives.

There are two procedures in examining the effectiveness of the distractors in a multiple – choice item. The first procedure requires that answers to the different distractors to be counted for the upper and lower groups. Good distractors are those chosen more frequently by students/participants from the lower group. When particular distractor is selected more frequently by those from the upper group, the researcher/teacher has to revise it. The analysis of distractors may also reveal some chosen by no one in either of the two groups of students. Such distractors should therefore be revised to make them more useful. An illustration of the foregoing analysis is shown below.

| Item | Group | Responses | | | | |
|---|---|---|---|---|---|---|
| | | A | B | C | D | E |
| 1 | Upper | 0 | 3 | 12 | 5 | 5 |
| | Lower | 0 | 7 | 0 | 7 | 6 |

An examination of item 1 reveals that no one from the upper and lower groups chose distractor A. it has revised or changed. Distractor C needs to be revised to make popular with those in the lower group.

Another method of analyzing the effectiveness of distractors is by determining the mean score of the students who respond to each distractor, as well as that those who choose the correct answer. A good distractor has lower mean scores than those related to the correct response.

**Some tips for writing options for multiple choice type test are presented as follows.**

1. Incorrect options should be plausibly related to the problem. If the incorrect options are completely unrelated to the problem, the correct alternative can be easily spotted by the examinee.
2. Correct alternative should appear similarly in sentences or phrases construction as the other distractors. Sometimes correct answers are more lengthy than the incorrect ones which may present a clue to the examinee.
3. Alternative should be randomly presented in each item. Test developers often place the correct options at the middle rather than in the first or last positions.
4. Avoid using alternatives like "none of the above", "both a and b", none of these, etc.

**METHOD 2: The Pearson Product – Moment Correlation Method.** This item analysis technique is used for test of continuous scaling with three (3) or more scale points. The Likert scales or bipolar scales are of this kind. There is a total score which serves as an X criterion and an item score which serves as an X criterion and an item score which is the Y criterion. This is done to each of all items. Therefore, if the draft consists of 60 items, there should be 60 correlation coefficients computed. Significant coefficient reflects good items while insignificants one reflect poor items. Most researchers consider a coefficient of .30 and above as indicating good items. Here is an illustration of this technique:

**Item No. 4:** Science is actually based on the best available evidence at the time; it may change with new evidence.

**1- Strongly Agree**
**2- Agree**
**3- Disagree**
**4- Strongly Disagree**

This is item No. 4 of a test which is a 4 -point type composed of 60 items, hence the scoring assigns 4, 3, 2 or 1 point to each item.

Let us suppose that there are 10 subjects tested in the trial run. The coefficient of correlation can be computed from these hypothetical data.

| **Subjects** | **X (Total Score)** | **Y (Item Score)** |
|---|---|---|
| A | 50 | 4 |
| B | 48 | 4 |
| C | 45 | 3 |
| D | 45 | 3 |
| E | 42 | 4 |
| F | 40 | 3 |
| G | 40 | 4 |
| H | 38 | 4 |
| I | 34 | 2 |
| J | 30 | 2 |

$$r_{xy} = \frac{n\Sigma XY - \Sigma XY^2}{\sqrt{(n\Sigma X2(\Sigma X)2(nY^2 - (\Sigma Y)^2}}$$

**Where X** is observed data for independent variable
**Y** the observed data for the dependent variable
**n** is sample size (cases)
$r_{xy}$ degree of relationship X & Y

Using the formula for Pearson r, the coefficient for item No 4 is 0.66 indicating the item is very good items.

**METHOD 3: Point – Biserial Correlation Method**. This is applied to test with dichotomous scoring system. e.g. Yes/No, right/wrong, improved/not improved. Unlike in the Pearson r method, the Y criterion is scored either 1 or 0. Correlations between, the total scores and items scores are tested. Items with low coefficient are considered poor and are usually discarded or revised.

**METHOD 4: Criterion of Internal Consistency Method.** Likert (1967) observed that item analysis is quite laborious so that he tried a simpler method in determining the internal consistency of an attitude scale. The results obtained were comparable with the results of item analysis using the Pearson correlation method. Based on these results, he suggested the use of simpler method since the criterion of internal consistency is mush easier to use and it yield essentially the same results. This is somewhat similar to the U-L Index Method, in that two criterion groups, the high group and the low group, are employed to judge the discriminatory power of an item. However, in this method. Likert recommends the use of the high 10 percent and below 10 percent groups.

The method has two purposes. First, it checks upon the correct assignment of numerical values. If the numerical values are reversed on a particular statement the extreme high group will score low on the that item and the extreme low group will score high. Hence, a negative difference (D) will be obtained item is differentiating or not. If it is not, then the high and the low group. Hence, the high group will not score appreciably higher than the low group in the statement. The term "appreciably" however, was not defined by Likert quantitatively. It looks like the direction is left to the test developer to "judge" which items are glaringly undifferentiating. Let's look at the table below to study an illustration of this method.

**A Hypothetical Illustration of an Application of the Criterion of Internal Consistency Method (N=50)**

| High 10% | TEST ITEMS (4 – Point Scale) | | | | | | | | | |
|---|---|---|---|---|---|---|---|---|---|---|
| | **1** | **2** | **3** | **4** | **5** | **6** | **7** | **8** | **9** | **10** |
| **1** | 4 | 4 | 4 | 4 | 4 | 3 | 4 | 2 | 4 | 3 |
| **2** | 4 | 2 | 4 | 2 | 2 | 4 | 4 | 2 | 4 | 3 |
| **3** | 4 | 4 | 4 | 4 | 4 | 4 | 4 | 1 | 3 | 3 |
| **4** | 4 | 4 | 4 | 4 | 2 | 4 | 4 | 2 | 4 | 4 |
| **5** | 3 | 4 | 4 | 3 | 4 | 3 | 2 | 2 | 4 | 4 |
| **Sum of High Group** | 19 | 18 | 20 | 17 | 16 | 18 | 18 | 9 | 19 | 17 |
| **Sum of** | | | | | | | | | | |

| Low Group | 17 | 8 | 9 | 8 | 18 | 10 | 11 | 18 | 11 | 10 |
|---|---|---|---|---|---|---|---|---|---|---|
| **Difference** | 2 | 10 | 11 | 9 | -2 | 8 | 7 | -9 | 8 | 7 |
| **Rank** | 8 | 2 | 1 | 3 | 9 | 4.5 | 6.5 | 10 | 4.5 | 6.5 |
| **Low 10%** | | | | | | | | | | |
| 46 | 4 | 1 | 1 | 2 | 3 | 2 | 3 | 4 | 3 | 2 |
| 47 | 4 | 1 | 2 | 2 | 4 | 2 | 2 | 3 | 3 | 2 |
| 48 | 3 | 2 | 2 | 1 | 3 | 3 | 1 | 4 | 2 | 2 |
| 49 | 3 | 2 | 2 | 1 | 4 | 2 | 3 | 4 | 2 | 2 |
| 50 | 3 | 2 | 2 | 2 | 4 | 1 | 2 | 3 | 1 | 2 |

It can be gleaned from the table above the items 2, 3, 4, 6, 7, 9 and 10 are differentiating items. The differences between the two extreme groups in these items are "appreciably" high therefore they can be included in the final draft of the scale. Item 1 and 5, however, are poor items while item 8 should be inspected more closely in terms of the numerical values assigned to the item scale. Reveals of the scaling may solve the problem of retaining or not retaining the item.

**METHOD 4: Use of the t-Test**. An alternative technique for item analysis is the use of the independent t-test. Previous try -outs, however, reveal that the use of the corelated or dependent t-test yields similar results. The simpler test which is the latter is thus suggested for this purpose. The use of this method is basically the same as the method just described above. It also makes use of two criterion groups, 10 percent high group and 10 percent low group. Mean differences between the two groups in each of the items are analyzed and determined whether the obtained t is statistically significant or not. Significant t-ratio indicate a good discriminatory index of the items while t-ratios indicate a good discriminatory index of the items while t -ratios which are not significant warrant rejection of the items.

Presentation of the analysis can be presented in a summary table seen below.

**ITEM ANALYSIS TABLE USING THE t-test**

| Items No. | Mean of High 10% | Mean of Low 10% | Differences | t-ratio | Decision |
|---|---|---|---|---|---|
| 1 | 3.5 | 3.0 | 0.5 | 1.60 | Reject |
| 2 | 3.3 | 3.2 | 0.1 | 1.42 | Reject |
| 3 | 4.2 | 2.0 | 2.2 | 2.89** | Retain |
| 4 | 3.0 | 1.8 | 1.2 | 2.22 | Retain |
| 5 | 4.1 | 2.1 | 2.0 | 2.0 | Retain |

* <.05
**p <.01

**METHOD 6: The Use of Two or More Techniques.** Although item analysis is laborious, some researchers have opted to play safe by going through this process. Others even use two or three techniques simultaneously to ensure more accurate quantitative judgement.

**STEP 5: Second Run or Final Test Administration.** More often than not, the second trial run becomes the final run. This mean that the second trial run you may now administer the draft resulting from the item analysis to your final sample. The test items at this point may have been reduced considerably, and a check at the proportions initially planned in the TOS is again necessary. It may be wise to compare the original TOS with the proportion of items left in the final draft to find out if the emphasis originally planned is maintained in the final draft. Necessary adjustments can still be done before finally administering the instrument to the final sample.

**STEP 6: Evaluation of the Test.** After the final run, the test can now be evaluated statistically in terms of its validity and reliability.

1. **Evaluating the Test Validity.** Validity - refers to the extent to which the instrument measures what it intends to measure and performs as it is designed to perform. It is unusual and nearly impossible that an instrument is 100% valid that is why validity is generally measured in degrees. As a process, validation involves collecting and analyzing data to assess the accuracy of an instrument. There are numerous statistical tests and measures to assess the validity of quantitative instruments that generally involves pilot testing. There are three major types of validity. These are the following.
    a) **Criterion- related validity** is achieved by determining the effectiveness of the test to measure results against a given set of criteria or standards. In achievement or performance test, the desired competencies are used as the criteria. This type of validity is better understood statistically. A criterion is any other instrument that measures the same variable. Correlations can be conducted to determine the extent to which the different instruments measure the same variable. Criterion validity is measured in three ways:
    b) **Convergent validity** - shows that an instrument is highly correlated with instruments measuring similar variables. Example: geriatric suicide correlated significantly and positively with depression, loneliness and hopelessness.
    c) **Divergent validity** - shows that an instrument is poorly correlated to instruments that measure different variables. Example: there should be a low correlation between an instrument that measures motivation and one that measure self - efficacy.
    d) **Predictive validity** - means that the instrument should have high correlation with future criterions. Example: a score of high self- efficacy related to performing a task that should predict the likehood a participant

completing the task.

e) **Construct validity** refers to whether you can draw inferences about test scores related to the concept being studied. The extent of a test to appropriate its ability to demonstrate a theoretical construct or development characteristics or indicator is described by the materials' construct validity. There are three types of evidence that can be used to demonstrate a research instrument has construct validity:
   - **Homogeneity** - this means that the instrument measure one construct.
   - **Convergence** - this occurs when the instrument measures concept similar to that of other instruments. Although if there are no similar instruments available this will not be possible to do.
   - **Theory evidence** - this is evident when behavior is similar to theoretical proposition of the construct measured in the instrument.

**Some Common Test Validity**

a) **Aiken 's V (1985) Content – Validity Coefficient –** it is a calculation of the index of content validity based on the result of the assessment of several experts against an item in terms of the extent to how much the item represents the measured domain or construct. Aiken uses the calculation formula $V = S / [n (c-1)]$, where V is the value of the validity coefficient of Aiken, S is the value of the rating scale minus 1, n is the number of assessors or experts used in the validation, and c is the highest score in the rating scale.

| **Aiken V Content Validity Coefficient** | |
|---|---|
| **Scale** | **Interpretation** |
| $V< 0.4$ | Not Valid |
| $0.4 \leq v \leq 0.8$ | Valid |
| $v > 0.8$ | Strongly Valid |

**Illustrative Example of Test of Validity using Aiken 's V Content – Validity Coefficient**

b) **CVR Lawshe's Content – Validity Coefficient** – is a linear

| | TEST ITEMS | | | | | | | | | | | | | | | | | | | |
|---|---|---|---|---|---|---|---|---|---|---|---|---|---|---|---|---|---|---|---|---|
| RATER | 1 | S1 | 2 | S2 | 3 | S3 | 4 | S4 | 5 | S5 | 6 | S6 | 7 | S7 | 8 | S8 | 9 | S9 | 10 | S10 |
| A | 4 | 3 | 4 | 3 | 4 | 3 | 4 | 3 | 4 | 3 | 4 | 3 | 4 | 3 | 4 | 3 | 4 | 3 | 4 | 3 |
| B | 4 | 3 | 4 | 3 | 3 | 2 | 4 | 3 | 3 | 2 | 4 | 3 | 4 | 3 | 3 | 2 | 3 | 2 | 3 | 2 |
| C | 3 | 2 | 4 | 3 | 4 | 3 | 4 | 3 | 3 | 2 | 4 | 3 | 4 | 3 | 4 | 3 | 4 | 3 | 4 | 3 |
| D | 4 | 3 | 4 | 3 | 4 | 3 | 4 | 3 | 3 | 2 | 4 | 3 | 4 | 3 | 4 | 3 | 4 | 3 | 4 | 3 |
| ΣS | | 11 | | 12 | | 11 | | 12 | | 9 | | 12 | | 12 | | 11 | | 11 | | 11 |
| N | | 4 | | 4 | | 4 | | 4 | | 4 | | 4 | | 4 | | 4 | | 4 | | 4 |
| C | | 4 | | 4 | | 4 | | 4 | | 4 | | 4 | | 4 | | 4 | | 4 | | 4 |
| C-1 | | 3 | | 3 | | 3 | | 3 | | 3 | | 3 | | 3 | | 3 | | 3 | | 3 |
| N (C-1 ) | | 12 | | 12 | | 12 | | 12 | | 12 | | 12 | | 12 | | 12 | | 12 | | 12 |
| V | | 0.92 | | 1.00 | | 0.92 | | 1.00 | | 0.75 | | 1.00 | | 1.00 | | 0.92 | | 0.92 | | 0.92 |
| Interpretation | | Strongly Valid | | Strongly Valid | | Strongly Valid | | Strongly Valid | | Strongly Valid | | Strongly Valid | | Strongly Valid | | Strongly Valid | | Strongly Valid | | Strongly Valid |

transformation of a proportional level of agreement on how many "experts" within a panel rate an item "essential". A CV ratio (CVR) is a numeric value indicating the instrument's degree of validity determined from expert's ratings of CV. One rule of thumb suggests that a CVR of at least 0.78 is necessary to deem an item or scale as valid.

$$CVR = \frac{n_e - (N/2)}{N/2}$$

where CVR is the content validity ratio, $n_e$ is the number of panel members indicating an item "essential," and N is the number of panel members. Lawshe (1975) suggested the transformation (from proportion to CVR) was of worth as it could readily be seen whether the level of agreement among panel members was greater than 50%. CVR values range between −1 (perfect disagreement) and +1 (perfect agreement) with CVR values above zero indicating that over half of panel members agree an item essential. However, when interpreting a CVR for any given item, it may be important to consider whether the level of agreement is also above that which may have occurred by chance. Acceptable standard for the S-CVI recommended a minimum S-CVI of .80. If the I-CVI is higher than 79%, the item will be appropriate. If it is between 70% and 79%, it needs revision. If it is less than 70% it is eliminated.

Minimum values of content validity ratio and one-tailed test, P = 0.05

| Number of panelists | Minimum value | Number of panelists | Minimum value |
|---|---|---|---|
| 5 | 0.99 | 11 | 0.59 |
| 6 | 0.99 | 12 | 0.56 |
| 7 | 0.99 | 13 | 0.54 |
| 8 | 0.75 | 14 | 0.51 |
| 9 | 0.78 | 15 | 0.49 |
| 10 | 0.62 | 20 | 0.42 |

**Illustrative Example of Test of Validity using CVR Lawshe's Content – Validity Coefficient**

| Test Item No. | Expert 1 | Expert 2 | Expert 3 | Expert 4 | Expert 5 | CVR |
|---|---|---|---|---|---|---|
| Item 1 | x | X | x | X | | 0.6 |
| Item 2 | x | X | x | X | x | 1 |
| Item 3 | x | X | x | X | x | 1 |
| Item 4 | x | X | x | X | x | 1 |
| Item 5 | x | X | x | X | x | 1 |
| Item 6 | x | X | x | X | x | 1 |
| CVR(Critical) for a panel size (N) of 5 is 1. | | | | | | 0.933 |

Legend: (x) where essential, blank where not essential

c) **Cohen's kappa statistic** measures interrater reliability (sometimes called interobserver agreement). Interrater reliability, or precision, happens when your data raters (or collectors) give the same score to the same data item. In addition, Cohen's Kappa has the assumption that the raters are deliberately chosen. If your raters are chosen at random from a population of raters, use Fleiss' kappa instead.

where:
$P_o$ = the relative observed agreement among raters.
$P_e$ = the hypothetical probability of chance agreement

$$\kappa = \frac{p_o - p_e}{1 - p_e} = 1 - \frac{1 - p_o}{1 - p_e},$$

| Value of Kappa Index | Interpretation |
|---|---|
| Less than 0 | Very weak |
| 0.00 – 0.20 | Weak |
| 0.21 – 0.40 | Medium Weak |
| 0.41 – 0.60 | Medium |
| 0.61 – 0.80 | Good |
| 0.81 – 1.00 | Very good |

**The Kappa Index Value and Interpretation**

**Illustrative Example of Test of Validity using Cohen's kappa statistic**

| RATER 1 | RATER 2 |
|---|---|
| 0 | 0 |
| 0 | 0 |
| 1 | 0 |
| 0 | 0 |
| 1 | 1 |
| 0 | 0 |
| 1 | 1 |
| 0 | 0 |
| 1 | 1 |
| 1 | 1 |

| | | | | | RCENTAGE |
|---|---|---|---|---|---|
| RATER 1 | 0 | | | | 60% |
| RATER 2 | 1 | | | | 40% |
| | TOTAL | 5 | 5 | 10 | |
| | PERCENTAGE | 50% | 50% | | |

| | |
|---|---|
| $p_o$ | 0.90 |
| $p_e$ | 0.50 |
| k | 0.8 |
| Interpretation | Good |

## RESEARCH INSTRUMENT VALIDATION SHEET

Name of Validator:
Degree/Specialization:
Position/Designation:

**RESEARCH TITLE:**

**Direction:** This tool asks for your evaluation of the questionnaire to be used in data gathering for the investigation stated above, to established its validity. You are requested to give your honest assessment using the criteria stated below; Plese check (✓) only one from the selection.

| Scale | Interprettaion | Description |
|---|---|---|
| 4 | Highly Valid | The questionnaire is valid and can provide unbiased data for investigation, allowing 0 – 5% error. |
| 3 | Valid | The questionnaire is valid and can provide unbiased data for investigation, allowing 6 - 10% error. |
| 2 | Less Valid | The questionnaire is valid and can provide unbiased data for investigation, allowing 11 – 20% error. |
| 1 | Not Valid at all | The questionnaire is valid and can provide unbiased data for investigation, allowing more than 20% error. |

| Indicators | 4 | 3 | 2 | 1 |
|---|---|---|---|---|
| **Clarity and Direction of Items.**<br>a)<br>b) The vocabulary level, language & structure are at the conceptual level of the particpants/respondents.<br>c) The test directions and the items are written in a clear and understandable manner. | ☒ | ☐ | ☐ | ☐ |
| **Presentation and Organization of Items.**<br>The items are presented and organized in a logical manner. | ☒ | ☐ | ☐ | ☐ |
| **Suitability of Items.**<br>**a)** The items appropriately presented the substance/content of the research.<br>**b)** The questions/items are designed to determine what are supposed to be measured. | ☒ | ☐ | ☐ | ☐ |
| **Adequateness of the Content.**<br>The number of the questions/items per domain/area is representative enough of all questions needed for the research. | ☐ | ☐ | ☐ | ☐ |
| **Attainment of the Purpose.**<br>The instrument as a whole can fulfill the objectives needed for the research. | ☒ | ☐ | ☐ | ☐ |

| | | | | |
|---|---|---|---|---|
| **Objective.** Each item question/indicator requires only one specific answer or measures only one behavior. | ☒ | ☐ | ☐ | ☐ |
| **Scale and Evaluation of Rating.** The scale adapted/used is appropriate for the item/indicator. | ☒ | ☐ | ☐ | ☐ |

**Comments and Suggestions:**

| |
|---|
| |

______________________________

**(NAME OF VALIDATOR)**
**Signature over printed name of validator**

**Sample Certification of Validation**

# CERTIFICATION OF VALIDATION

This is to certify that the research tools for the thesis entitled "***Title of Research***" prepared and submitted by ***Name of Researchers*** from "***Name of Institution***", ***Name of Department*** had undergone validation. It is furthered certified that after considering all recommendations and suggestions for the improvement of the said research tools, has been evaluated and found aligned to the statement of the problem, research questions, theoretical-conceptual framework of the study that conform to the required standard for scholarly research, the undersigned have recommended the use of this research tools for the data collection.

**CERTIFIED BY**

____________________________________

**Name of Validator**
(Name of Institution)
**Validator**

2. **Evaluating the test of Reliability** relates to the extent to which the instrument is consistent. The instruments should be able to obtain the same response when applied to respondents who are similarly situated. Likewise, when instrument is applied at two different points in time, the responses must highly correlate with one another. Hence reliability can be measured by correlate the responses of subjects exposed to the instrument at two different time periods or by correlating the responses of the subjects who are situated. An example of this is when a participant completing an instrument meant to measure motivation should have approximately the same responses each time the test is completed. Although it is not possible to give an exact calculation of reliability, an estimate of reliability can be achieved through different measures. The three attributes of reliability are the following:
   a) **Internal consistency or homogeneity** is when an instrument measures a specific concept. This concept is through question or indicators and each question must correlate highly with the total for this dimension. There are four ways to check the internal consistency or homogeneity of the index.
      - ✓ In **alternate - form reliability,** at least two forms of test on a subject matter are prepared and administered once to a common group. The

test results are also subjected to test of correlation. The computed coefficient correlation becomes the reliability index.

- ✓ In **split - half reliability,** the material is administered also one to a group of test - takers. The results are splits into halves and these are compared. A test of relationship is calculated using the Spearman - Brown formula. The index of reliability results from this calculation
- ✓ The **inter - rater or scorer reliability** is another measure of reliability, where at least two scorers separately review and score a set of sampled test papers. Their independent scores are tested for relationship. The resulting coefficient of correlation becomes the inter - rater reliability index.
- ✓ The **inter - item correlation** is based on a single form and administration of the test. Kuder - Richardson formula is used in calculating the inter - item reliability index of the test.

**b) Stability or test - retest correlation** this is an aspect of reliability where many researchers report that a highly reliable test indicates that the test is stable over time. Test - retest correlation provides an indication of stability over time. It is an extent to which scores on a test are essentially invariant over time. This definition clearly focuses on the measurement instrument and the obtained test scores in terms of test - retest stability. An example of this is when we ask the respondents in our sample the four questions once in the month of September and again in December. We can examine whether the two waves of the same measures yield similar results.

**c) Equivalence reliability** is measured by the correlation of scores between different versions of the same instruments or between instruments that measure the same or similar constructs, such that one instrument can be reproduced by the other. If we want to know the extent to which different investigators use the same instrument to measure the same individuals at the same time yield consistent results. Equivalence may also be estimated by measuring the same concepts with different instruments, for example, survey questionnaire and official records, on the same sample, which is known as multiple - forms reliability.

Kothari (2004) suggested that reliability can be improved in the following two ways.

- By standardizing the conditions under which the measurement takes place i.e., we must ensure that external sources of variation such as boredom, fatigue, etc., are minimized to the extent possible. That will improve stability aspect.
- By carefully designed directions for measurement with no variation from group to group, by using trained and motivated persons to conduct the research and also by broadening the sample of items used. This will improve equivalence aspect.

## Common Test of Reliability

**Cronbach's alpha,** α (or coefficient alpha), developed by Lee Cronbach in 1951, measures reliability, or internal consistency. "Reliability" is another name for consistency.

Cronbach's alpha tests to see if multiple-question Likert scale surveys are reliable. These questions measure latent variables—hidden or unobservable variables like: a person's conscientiousness, neurosis or openness. These are very difficult to measure in real life. Cronbach's alpha will tell you how closely related a set of test items are as a group.

$$\alpha = \frac{N \cdot \bar{c}}{\bar{v} + (N-1) \cdot \bar{c}}$$

Where:

N = the number of items.
c̄ = average covariance between item-pairs.
v̄ = average variance.

## Rule of Thumb for Results

A rule of thumb for interpreting alpha for dichotomous questions (i.e. questions with two possible answers) or Likert scale questions is:

| Cronbach's alpha | Internal consistency |
|---|---|
| $\alpha \geq 0.9$ | Excellent |
| $0.9 > \alpha \geq 0.8$ | Good |
| $0.8 > \alpha \geq 0.7$ | Acceptable |
| $0.7 > \alpha \geq 0.6$ | Questionable |
| $0.6 > \alpha \geq 0.5$ | Poor |
| $0.5 > \alpha$ | Unacceptable |

## Threats to Construct Validity

1. **Hypothesis Guessing.** This threat is when the subject guesses the intent of the test and consciously, or subconsciously, alters their behavior. It does not matter whether they guess the hypothesis correctly, only that their behavior changes.
2. **Evaluation Apprehension**. This particular threat is based upon the tendency of humans to act differently when under pressure. Individual

testing is notorious for bringing on an adrenalin rush, and this can improve or hinder performance. In this respect, evaluation apprehension is related to ecological external validity, where it affects the process of generalization.

3. **Poor Construct Definition.** Researcher Expectancies and Bias. Researchers are only human and may give cues that influence the behavior of the subject. Humans give cues through body language, and subconsciously smiling when the subject gives a correct answer, or frowning at an undesirable response, all have an effect. This effect can lower construct validity by clouding the effect of the actual research variable. To reduce this effect, interaction should be kept to a minimum, and assistants should be unaware of the overall aims of the project.
4. **Construct Confounding**. Construct validity is all about semantics and labeling. Defining a construct in too broad or too narrow terms can invalidate the entire experiment. For example, a researcher might try to use job satisfaction to define overall happiness. This is too narrow, as somebody may love their job but have an unhappy life outside the workplace. Equally, using general happiness to measure happiness at work is too broad. Many people enjoy life but still hate their work! Mislabeling is another common definition error: stating that you intend to measure depression, when you actually measure anxiety, compromises the research. The best way to avoid this particular threat is with good planning and seeking advice before you start your research program.
5. **Interaction of Different Treatments**. This threat to construct validity occurs when other constructs mask the effects of the measured construct. For example, self-esteem is affected by self-confidence and self-worth. The effect of these constructs needs to be incorporated into the research.
6. **Unreliable Scores**. This particular threat is where more than one treatment influences the final outcome. he constructs validity is now too low for the results to have any meaning. Only good planning and monitoring of the subjects can prevent this.
7. **Mono-Operation Bias.** Variance in scores is a very easy trap to fall into.
8. **Mono-Method Bias.** This threat involves the independent variable, and is a situation where a single manipulation is used to influence a construct
9. This threat to construct validity involves the dependent variable, and occurs when only a single method of measurement is used.

## Illustrative Example of Research Instrument

**CoSIM (Comics cum SIM): An Innovative Material in Teaching Biology (Samosa, 2021)**

### Research Instruments

The instruments used in the study was a researcher-made instruments includes the researcher-made pretest-posttest, attitude survey toward utilization of CoSIM as an innovative material in teaching photosynthesis were carefully chosen and improved after several consultations and discussions with the science experts from the academe. Important points were chosen that could necessarily represent the essence, substance, and intention of the study. The first draft of the instruments will be submitted to the science experts for comments, suggestions, and recommendation to improve its presentation. Each item in the instruments was carefully checked and the whole content of the instrument was submitted to the science experts to establish its reliability and validity, it will be piloted to 30 respondents and run in the computation program for test reliability and validity.

The following are the instrument to be used in the research study.

**Strategic Intervention Materials Strategic Intervention Material (SIM)** is one of the intervention materials that can be used to promote active learning in the classroom. SIM is designed to help students a needed support to increase and deepen their skills, knowledge and understanding from concrete science to what is more abstract.

**Photosynthesis Achievement tests (PAT)** this test was designed by the researcher. It contained forty (50) multiple choice response test. This was administered before the treatment and after the treatment. The test was used as pre – test and post-test. The (PAT) was to measure the learners" ability to recall, relate, and apply any of information received during the treatment. Based on the test-retest reliability revealed it was acceptable with computed value of .703.

**Attitude Survey Attitude Survey** is used to measure the extent of effectiveness of SIMs in Learning the Concepts of photosynthesis based on the learners perceive experience towards the innovation. The attitude survey composed of 14- items of 4- Likert scale survey. Using the CVR - Lawshe"s Content – Validity Coefficient revealed that attitude survey was acceptable based on the computed CVR of 0.829.

## Data Collection Methods

Data collection is a process of collecting information from all the relevant sources to find answers to the research problem, test the hypothesis and evaluate the outcomes. Data collection methods can be divided into two categories: secondary methods of data collection and primary methods of data collection.

1. **Secondary Data Collection Methods.** It is a type of data that has already been published in books, newspapers, magazines, journals, online portals etc. There is an abundance of data available in these sources about your research area in business studies, almost regardless of the nature of the research area. Therefore, application of appropriate set of criteria to select secondary data to be used in the study plays an important role in terms of increasing the levels of research validity and reliability. These criteria include, but not limited to date of publication, credential of the author, reliability of the source, quality of discussions, depth of analyses, the extent of contribution of the text to the development of the research area etc.
2. **Primary Data Collection Methods.**

   Primary data collection methods can be divided into two groups: quantitative and qualitative.

   a) **Quantitative data collection methods** are based in mathematical calculations in various formats. Methods of quantitative data collection and analysis include questionnaires with closed-ended questions, methods of correlation and regression, mean, mode and median and others. Quantitative methods are cheaper to apply, and they can be applied within shorter duration of time compared to qualitative methods. Moreover, due to a high level of standardization of quantitative methods, it is easy to make comparisons of findings.

   b) **Qualitative research methods**, on the contrary, do not involve numbers or mathematical calculations. Qualitative research is closely associated with words, sounds, feeling, emotions, colors and other elements that are non-quantifiable. Qualitative studies aim to ensure greater level of depth of understanding and qualitative data collection methods include interviews, questionnaires with open-ended questions, focus groups, observation, game or role-playing, case studies etc.

## Common Data Collection Methods

1. **Questionnaire -** The questionnaire is the commonly used instrument for collecting research data from the participants of a study. It basically seeks the opinions of individuals in a sample or a population on issues directly related to the objectives of the research study. The questionnaire consists of a set of structured and unstructured questions designed by researchers to obtain data

from the respondents. No research is better than its questionnaire and a faulty questionnaire means faulty research. Hence, a questionnaire designed must be valid, reliable and must not be bogus so that the data collected can validate the research. Questionnaire has many advantages which include anonymity of the respondents is guaranteed; it facilitates the collection of large amounts of data in a relatively short period and it is cheap to administer. The major demerit of the method is that some confusing and misleading questions cannot be clarified as the researcher may not be there to explain the questions, and also, sometimes, the questions may not be easily comprehensible to individuals who are illiterate, thus, the method is restricted only to educated respondents. Moreover, the characteristics of a good questionnaire consist of:

a) Questions should not be ambiguous. This implies that it must be capable of only one interpretation.
b) Questions must be easily understood.
c) Questions should be capable of having a precise answer.
d) Questions must not contain words of vague meaning.
e) Questions should not require rigorous calculations.
f) Questions should not require the respondent to decide upon classification.
g) Questions must not be in such a form that the answers will be biased.
h) The questionnaire should not be too long.
i) It should not be too wordy.
j) The questionnaire should cover the exact object of the inquiry.

2. **Interview** - is a measurement instrument otherwise known as oral questionnaire. It involves a process where a researcher solicits information from respondents through verbal interaction. A researcher would have previously prepared a schedule list of structured questions pertinent to the study before meeting respondents for their opinions on a subject matter. The researcher poses questions to the respondents and the answers are recorded by the researcher. Materials that could be used during interview period include tape recorder, paper and biro. The major advantage of this method is that it produces high response rate. Besides, it tends to be representative of the entire population of the study, and personal contact between the researcher and respondents enables the researcher to explain confusing and ambiguous questions in detail. However, its disadvantages include interviewer's bias; inaccessibility to wealthy respondents due to fear of insecurity and the amount of data that can be collected through this method is usually limited compare to questionnaire method. Interview can be conducted personally or through telephone or electronic mailing system.
3. **Observation** - This is an instrument that is employed by a researcher in which an individual behavior or situation is observed and recorded. There are two types of observation: participant observation and non-participant observation.

In participant observation, the researcher is a member of the group to be observed. Here, accurate and timely result would be obtained by the researcher, but it has the problem of biasness. Non-participant observation on the other hand, the researcher is not a member of the group to be observed. Here, the result will be viable as it is free from being biased but it has the problem of inaccuracy and delayed result. Both observation methods enhance firsthand information, flexible and cheaper to carryout, demand less active cooperation of the observed and their results are reliable for research activity. However, observation method is popular tool in research especially in behavioral and social sciences; the authors argue that it requires special skills to make and assess behavioral observation in research. In carrying out behavioral observation, first thing to do is to develop behavioral categories (coding scheme). This involves identifying specific attributes that will give clues to the problem at hand. The authors further reiterated that researchers may observe the following guidelines when developing observation method:

a) "Clearly define the goal of the instrument;
b) Carry out preliminary observations of your subjects under the conditions that will prevail during the study with the aim of identifying behaviors exhibited by the subjects; and
c) Construct a complete list of the identified behavior. Also, behavioral categories can also be developed through literature search. These will provide opportunity to determine whether a similar study had previously been conducted. The result of such similar study may be adopted or adapted in the present study.

4. **Focus Group Discussion: -** This data collection instrument refers to a process whereby researchers obtain data from large group of people at the same time. This method is different from interview method; in an interview method, researcher focuses on one person at a time but in a focus group discussion method, the researcher obtains data from large number (group) of people for his research activity. Focus group discussion method is very popular when carrying out research in the field of behavioral science, library and information science, archival science, records, and information technology. It could be noted here that a need may arise for a researcher to use more than 2 or 3 approaches to obtain data for his research activity. This depends on the supervisor, nature of the research or problem to be investigated.

However, in focus group discussion; a researcher identifies key informants that may be contacted to elicit the deserved information on the variable(s) of interest in a study. It is very important to note that in evaluator study or when accessing the performance of a system or a project or when working at a policy and its impact on a particular operation in a society or organization; focus group discussion method could employed. The approach is used to generate qualitative data in explaining a phenomenon under study or investigation. Membership of the focus group discussion should not exceed 10 members at a

time. It is like a mini conference where members of a group could be assembled in a conducive location. Before now, it is needful for the researcher to have obtained their consent to take part in the study. Besides, the researcher must design a focus group discussion guide. The guide must contain outlines that capture variables of interest in the study.
The following materials are needed for this method of data collection:

- Research assistants;
- Video recorder and cassette;
- Biro and paper;
- Tape recorder and cassette, and
- Light refreshment to entertain the participants.

After the focus group discussion exercise, the researcher has to transcribe the data into qualitative information e.g. on the nature of reference services available in the library; in a group where 10 members are involved, if 7 members affirmed that they are having good reference services in their library while the rest members' response are negative. Then it can be calculated/quantify as: 7/10 *100 = 70%; this is the figure that the researcher will report in his work. Moreover, the major advantage of this method is that it added credibility and originality to the research activity while it challenges include: too cost to carry out, it takes too much of time to conduct and some of the respondents may not be free to contribute extensively especially if their boss is invited to such gathering.

**5. Experiment**

This type of data collection instrument takes place in pure and applied science research. Here the researchers carry out some experiments in the laboratory setting to test some reactions that may take place in the object of research. The advantages of this method are that it produces immediate result, its results are viable and error free if it is well carrying out under normal condition/circumstances. While its problems include it is too costly to undertake and those chemicals used may cause permanent damage to the researcher if they are carelessly handled.

**6. Photovoice**

Photovoice is a participatory method that enables people to identify, represent and enhance their community, life circumstances or engagement with a programme through photography and accompanying written captions. Photovoice involves giving a group of participant's cameras, enabling them to capture, discuss and share stories they find significant.

**7. Picture Story**

The picture story method enables children, in a fun and participatory way, to communicate their perspectives on particular issues through a series of drawing (story telling) they have made. The story telling can either be done in writing, depending on the child's level of literacy, or verbally with a researcher. The picture story method is relatively quick and inexpensive, particularly if the draw – and – write technique is adopted. The picture story method provides a non – threatening way to explore children's views on particular issue (e.g. barrier to girl's education) and to begin to identify what can be done to address any struggles faced by children.

## Classification of Research Based on Data Collection Methods

| Types of Research | Data Collection Methods |
|---|---|
| Survey research | Questionnaire, focus group discussion, interview, and observation. |
| Correlational research | Observation, questionnaire, focus group discussion and interview |
| Evaluation research | Focus group discussion, interview, and observation |
| Experimental research | Experiment and observation |
| Action research | Questionnaire and interview |

## Illustrative Example of Data Collection/Gathering Procedures

**CoSIM (Comics cum SIM): An Innovative Material in Teaching Biology (Samosa, 2021)**

### Data Collection/Gathering Procedures

The data from the study were gathered using documentation procedure. This could be made possible by considering the details from the pretest-posttest and attitude test employed in the study. Upon the approval of the final draft of the instruments by the research experts, the researcher wrote a letter to the School Division Superintendent (SDS) for approval to conduct a research study on the effectiveness of CoSIM (Comics cum Strategic Intervention Material) to improve the academic performance of students in teaching the concepts of photosynthesis. Upon the approval and endorsement of the subject SDS, the researcher was all set to report to the School Head of the subject school for the actual conduct of the study. The content of the research study was assessed and evaluated until permission was hereby granted provided that no government funds shall be used during the conduct of the activity, classes will not be disrupted as indicated in DepED Order No. 9 s. 2005 re: "Instituting Measures to Increase Engaged Time-on-Task and Ensuring Compliance Therewith" and proper coordination with the school principal shall be arranged prior to the conduct of the said activity. Second, all participants will undergo pretested on basic concepts of photosynthesis. Secondly crafting and validation of CoSIM (Comics cum Strategic Intervention Material) and then will be submitted to LRMDS Coordinator for validation upon approved the materials the participants received CoSIM (Comics cum Strategic Intervention Material) as innovation. Third, all participants will undergo posttested and attitude survey towards the utilization of CoSIM as innovation to improve the academic performance of learners" in teaching the concepts of photosynthesis. Finally, was the Collation and Tabulation of Data. The researcher collated, tallied coded and tabulated all the information acquired from the subjects then analyzed and interpreted the statistical results.

## Ethical Considerations

Research, however novel its discoveries, is only of any value if it is carried out honestly. We cannot trust the results of a research project if we suspect that the researchers have not acted with integrity. Although it might be easy enough to take short cuts or even to cheat, it really is not worth it. Not only will your research be discredited when you are found out, but you will suffer severe penalties and humiliation.

It is a simple matter to follow the clear guidelines in citation that will prevent you being accused of passing off other people's work as your own – called plagiarism. In fact, to refer to or quote other people's work is seen as a virtue and demonstrates that you have read widely about your subject and are knowledgeable about the most important people and their ideas. Working with human participants in your research always raises ethical issues about how you treat them. People should be treated with respect, which has many implications for how exactly how you deal with them before, during and after the research. Educational and professional organizations who oversee research projects have strict ethical guidelines that must be followed. However, the issues can become quite complicated, with no clear-cut solutions. It is therefore important that you consult with others, especially advisers appointed for that purpose.

Even if you are not using human participants in your research, there is still the question of honesty in the way you collect, analyze and interpret data. By explaining exactly how you arrived at your conclusions you can avoid accusations of cover-ups or false reasoning.

There are two aspects of ethical issues in research

1. The individual values of the researcher relating to honesty and frankness and personal integrity.
2. The researcher's treatment of other people involved in the research, relating to informed consent, confidentiality, anonymity, and courtesy.

Although the principles underpinning ethical practice are fairly straightforward and easy to understand, their application can be quite difficult in certain situations. Not all decisions can be clear-cut in the realm of human relations.

According to Resnik (2007), in his article "What is ethics in Research & Why is it important?" explain importance of ethics in research. These are as follows:

1. Ethics promotes the pursuits of knowledge, truth, and credibility. It also fosters values that are essential to collaborative work. Research often

involves a great deal of cooperation and coordination among people in different filed or disciplines. The important values include trust, accountability, mutual respect, and fairness.

2. Many of the ethical norms ensure that researchers are held accountable to the public.
3. Adhere to ethical principles helps build public support for research. People are more likely to fund research studies that promote a variety of important moral and social values such as social responsibility, human right, animal right, and health and safety.

**Ethical Codes and Policies for Research**

Given the importance of ethics in the conduct of research, many professional associations, government agencies, and universities have come up with the following codes and policies for research.

1. **Honesty** - this must be maintained in all communication (e.g. when reporting data results, and procedures). Data should never be fabricated, falsified, or misrepresented.
2. **Objectivity** - biases should be avoided in the experimental design, data analysis, interpretation, expert testimony, and other aspects of research.
3. **Integrity** - consistency of thought and action is the foundation of the credibility of any research work. Promises and agreements should be kept, and all actions should be made with a sincere purpose.
4. **Care** - careless errors and negligence should be avoided. Your work and the work of your peers should be critically examined. Records of research activities be kept in good order and condition.
5. **Openness** - the researcher should be open to criticisms and new ideas. Research data results, ideas, and resources should also be shared with the public.
6. **Respect for intellectual property** - Proper acknowledgement should be given to all authors cited and sources in your research. Patents and copyrights should be recognized. Any published data, methods; result should not be used without permission. Credits should be given to where it is due.
7. **Confidentially** - Confidential communication or documents should be protected.
8. **Responsible publication** - the study should be done with the purpose of advancing research and scholarship. Wasteful and duplicate publication should be avoided.
9. Responsible mentoring - the research should seek to educate, mentor, and advise students.
10. **Respects for colleagues -** all peers should be treated fairly.

11. Social responsibility - social good should be promoted and social harm should be avoided.
12. **Non - discrimination** - all those eligible to participate in research should be allowed to do so.
13. **Competence** - Professional competence and expertise should be maintained and improved with the research.
14. **Legality** - A researcher should know and obey relevant laws, and institutional and government policies.
15. **Human subject protection** - Harms and risks to human lives should be minimized. Human dignity, privacy, and autonomy should be among the primary considerations of the research.

## Rights of Research Participants

The main purpose of a research is to produce results that would benefits the stakeholders in the study. Likewise, the participants are crucial elements of the research and they have the same right as the research beneficiaries. Some of the rights of research participants are as follows (Trochim, 2006; Smith; 2003; Polit, 2006).

1. **Voluntary participation** - any person should be coerced to participate in any research undertaking.
2. **Informed consent** - prospective research participants must be fully informed about the procedures and risks involved in the research. Their consent to participate must be secured.
3. **Risk harming** - participants should be protected from physical, financial, or psychological harm. The principle of non - maleficence states that is the researcher's duty to avoid, prevent, or minimize harm to the participants of the study.
4. **Confidentiality** - participants must be assured that their identity and other personal information will not be made available to anyone who is not directly involved in the study.
5. **Anonymity** - the participants must remain anonymous throughout the study even to the researchers themselves.

# RESEARCH SUBJECT INFORMED CONSENT FORM

**To the Prospective Research Subject:** Read this consent form carefully and ask many as you like before you decide whether you want to participate in this research study or not. You are free to ask questions at any time before, or after your participation in this research.

## Research Information

**Research Title:** Science Teacher's Competence and Behavior in the Conduct of Action Research: Basis for A Proposed Research Manual
**Research Name:** Resty C. Samosa

**Program/Degree:** Master of Arts in Teaching Science

**Institution:** University of Caloocan City

**Contact Number:** 09495676062

**Email Address:** resty.samosa002@deped.gov.ph

1. **Purpose:** You are being asked to participate in a research study designed to develop a research manual for science teachers. Specifically, the study aims to determine science teacher's competency and behavior in the conduct of action research in Schools Division of San Jose del Monte Bulacan.
2. **Procedures:** The purpose of answering the survey questionnaires via google form to obtain information on what constitutes on science teacher's competency, behavior and challenges in the conduct of action research.
3. **Possible Risks or Discomfort:** No known or possible risks can pose danger to you in any form as this research will only involve an answering the survey questionnaire. The survey, however, may consume a portion of your time. To lessen the possible inconvenience on your part, the survey will be done at a place most convenient to you.
4. **Possible Benefits:**
    - This will provide you the opportunity to work on your research understanding and be able to conduct action research to address problems encountered in the classroom.
    - The result of this study may be helpful in imbedding the coaching and mentoring on the utilization of crafted research manual to science teachers.

- The result of this study can serve as basis to encourage science teachers to submit action research proposal in the schools' division.
- This serves as a guide in designing and conducting teachers training/in-service training. This were increase the supervisory strategies that were help take an action in the teaching-learning areas in the school and the curriculum itself.
- This study will provide empirical data to address the need of action research manual at Schools Division of San Jose del Monte Bulacan. Through acquiring such data, would be able to conceptualize and implement programs and trainings for teachers relevant to research.

5. **Financial Considerations:** No additional cost on your part might result your participation in this study.
6. **Confidentiality:** Your identity in this study will be treated with outmost confidentiality. The results of the study or any other data may be published for scientific purposes but will not give your name or include any identifiable references to you. However, any records or data obtained as result of your participation in this study may be inspected by the person conducting this study, provided that such inspectors are legally obligated to protect any identifiable information from public disclosure, except where disclosure is otherwise required by law or court of competent jurisdiction. These records will be kept private insofar as permitted by laws.
7. **Termination of Research Study:** You are free to choose whether or not to participate in this study. There will be no penalty if you choose not to participate. You will be provided with any significant new findings developed during the course of this study that may relate to or influence your willingness to continue participation. In the event that you decide to discontinue your participation in this study, no fee shall be given to you.
8. **Available Information:** Any further questions you have about this study will be answered by the Principal Investigator:

   Name: Resty C. Samosa

   Contact Number:

   Email Address:
9. **Authorization:** I have read and understand this consent form, and I volunteer to participate in this research study. I understand that I will receive a copy of this form. I voluntarily choose to participate, but I understand that my consent does not take away any legal rights in the case of negligence or other legal fault of anyone who is involved in this study. I

further understand that nothing in this consent form is intended to replace any applicable laws.

______________________________________
**Participant's Signature Over Printed Name**

**Date:** ______________________________

**RESTY C. SAMOSA**
______________________________________
**Researcher's Signature Over Printed Name**

## Ethical Standards in Research Writings

It is a general notion that in the written work of any author, be it in books, magazines, research papers for a degree program, or even those papers which are to be submitted for funding programs, the reader assumes that the author is the sole originator of the written work, that any text or ideas borrowed from others are clearly identified as such by established scholarly convections, and that the ideas conveyed therein are accurately represented to the best of the author's abilities. For a writing to be considered ethical, it should be clear, accurate, fair, and honest (Kolin, as cited by Roig, 2006).

The following reminders must be taken into consideration for ethical research writing (Logan University, 2016):

1. Findings should be reported with complete honesty.
2. Intentional misinterpretation, misinformation, and misleading claims must be avoided.
3. Appropriate credits should be given when using other people's work.
4. Plagiarism should be avoided by fully acknowledging all content belonging to others.

## Plagiarism

It is the most widely recognized and one of the most serious violations of the contract between the reader and the writer (Roig, 2002). Plagiarism is the using of someone else's words or ideas and passing them off as your own. It can happen accidentally, for example if you are careless in your note - taking (University of Leicester, 2010). This can mean that you get mixed over what is an exact quote, and what you have written in your own words; or over was an idea of your own that you jotted down, or an idea from some text.

Research is a public trust that must be ethically conducted and so trustworthy and socially responsible if the results are to be valid and reliable. Roig (2002) states that plagiarism has been traditionally defined as the taking words, images, ideas, phrases, such as kidnapping of words, kidnapping of ideas, fraud, and literary theft. Plagiarism can manifest itself in a variety of ways and it is not just confined to student papers or published articles or books.

Plagiarism can take many forms. There are two major types in scholarly writing: plagiarism of ideas and plagiarism of text. Responsible authorship practices are an important part of research.

Plagiarism of ideas is "appropriating an idea (e.g., an explanation, a theory, a conclusion, a hypothesis, a metaphor) in whole or in part, or with superficial modifications without giving credits to its originator" (Roig, 2001). "Plagiarism is the appropriation of another person's ideas, processes, results, or words without giving appropriate credits, including those obtained through confidential review of others' research proposals and manuscripts. (Office of Science and Technology Policy, 1999).

The following are considered as acts of plagiarism (Cristobal & Cristobal, 2017).

1. Claiming authorship of a work or creation done by another person.
2. Copying entire written work or portion of it - including words, sentences, and ideas - without acknowledging the author.
3. Failing to put quotation marks to distinguish a quotation taken directly from a source.
4. Giving incorrect information about the source of a quotation.
5. Merely changing the words but retaining the sentence structure so that the selection or quotes still bears a resembles to the original source.
6. Using so many words and ideas from original that it makes up a large portion of your work, even if you acknowledge the original author.

Plagiarism should not be tolerated as the unauthorized use of original ideas and works constitute a violation of Intellectual property rights. The world Intellectual Property Organization has the following definition of Intellectual property.

"Intellectual property refers to creations of the mind: inventions; literary and artistic work; and symbols, names, and images used in commerce." (WIPO, 2004).

Intellectual property covers two categories: Industrial property, which includes patents, trademark s, and industrial designs, and copyright, which includes published works such as literary works, textbooks, reference books, and other artistic works such as creative design, film, music, radio broadcasts and performance art. Creators of such works and intellectual property are given rights and protections and the unauthorized use of intellectual property is subject to legal sanctions.

In the Philippines, intellectual property is protected by **Republic Act 8293** or the **Intellectual Property Code of the Philippines**. Following is the provision of the Code regarding published works:

> *"Published works" means works, which the consent of the authors, are made available to the public by wire or wireless means in such a way that members of the public may access these works from a place and time individually chosen by them: provided, that availability of such copies has been such, as to satisfy the reasonable requirements of the public, having regard to the nature of the work…*

Furthermore, the code also states the following provisions regarding copyright ownership,

> *178.1* *Subject to the provisions of these sections, in the case of original literary and artistic works, copyright shall belong to the author of the work;*
>
> *178. 2* *In the case of work of joint authorship, the co - authors shall be the original owners of the copyright, and in the absence of agreement, their rights shall be governed by the rules on co - ownership. If, however, a work of joint authorship consists of parts that can be used separately and the author of each part can be identified, the author of each part shall be original owner of the copyright in the part that he has created.*

This is the basis of ownership of any published article or materials in the form of books, magazines, and the like as well as those that are in electronic form. Using these materials, in part or, in commercial publications such as textbooks without recognizing the author or authors constitutes an infringement of copyright which has corresponding consequences. This acts states that in determining the number of years of imprisonment and the amount of fine, the court shall consider the value of the infringing materials that the defendant has produced or manufactures and the damage that the copying owner has suffered by reason of the infringement.

Copyright infringement and its corresponding sanctions, however, only apply to commercial use of intellectual property. In academic research, plagiarism and its related acts constitute academic dishonesty and may be cause for invalidation of a research study and other sanctions on the offenders. Educational institutions and academic organization have their own rules and sanctions such as failing grade in the course where such violation was committed, and in extreme cases, the revocation of a degree conferred.

Sharma and Singh (2011) list the following tips to avoid plagiarism.

1. Sufficient time should be allotted for writing

2. Hard copies of all relevant references should be cited.
3. All references should be read carefully, and its important parts should be highlighted.
4. Sufficient attribution should be placed when using the ideas of others.
5. Lines with factual details are to be referenced.
6. The appropriateness of inserting references should be determined.
7. Written permission should be acquired text and figures coped from other sources.
8. All the text should be paraphrased - that is, written by the author in his or her own language.
9. Copying and pasting text from sources while writing should be avoided. If one is not good typing, he or she can request from assistance from a typist.
10. Before submitting an article, all files, figures, and references should be prepared accordance to the prescribed standards.

**Fair use**

The Law, however, recognizes certain situation the use of copyrighted content is acceptable and constitutes as "fair use" of intellectual property. The intellectual Property Code identifies the following as acceptable use of intellectual property.

1. Use of works in the public domain. An intellectual property is considered to be in the public domain once the rights of the author have lapsed after a period defined by law (50 years after the death of the author).
2. Use of copyrighted work for criticism, comment, news reporting, teaching and classroom use, scholarship and research, and other similar purposes.
3. Reproduction of works as parts of reports on current news which broadcast to the public.
4. Use of works and materials from the government and its various branches, departments, and offices, if permission for use is acquired.

Although fair use gives academic researchers great freedoms in the selections and use of certain sources, due diligence should still be taken in citing the sources and informing the copyright owners regarding the use of their works.

## A. RESEARCHER INFORMATION

<table>
<tr><td colspan="2">RESEARCH TITLE:</td></tr>
<tr><td colspan="2">SHORT DESCRIPTION OF THE RESEARCH:</td></tr>
<tr><td>RESEARCH CATEGORY (Check <u>only</u> one)<br>☐ National<br>☐ Region<br>☐ Schools Division<br>☐ District<br>☐ School<br><br>(check <u>only one</u>)<br>☐ Applied Research<br>☐ Action Research</td><td>RESEARCH AGENDA CATEGORY (check only one main research theme)<br>☐ Teaching and Learning<br>☐ Child Protection<br>☐ Human Resource Development<br>☐ Governance<br><br>(check up to one cross-cutting theme, if applicable)<br><br>☐ DRRM<br>☐ Gender and Development<br>☐ Inclusive Education<br>☐ Others (please specify): ________</td></tr>
<tr><td>FUND SOURCE (e.g. BERF, SERF, others) *</td><td>AMOUNT</td></tr>
<tr><td>Personal Fund</td><td></td></tr>
<tr><td>TOTAL AMOUNT</td><td></td></tr>
</table>

## B. PROPONENT INFORMATION

| Last name | First name | Middle name |
|---|---|---|
| | | |
| Birthday | Sex | Designation |
| | | |
| Region/Division/School | | |
| Contact nos. | Email address: | |
| Educational Attainment<br>(Degree Title) | Title of Action Research: | |
| Signature of Proponent | | |

## IMMEDIATE SUPERVISOR'S CONFORME

I hereby endorse the attached research proposal. I certify that the proponent has the capacity to implement a research study without compromising her office functions.

________________________________________

Name and Signature of Immediate Supervisor
Position:
Date:

## DECLARATION OF ANTI – PLAGIARISM

1. I, **(Name of Researcher)** Underlined that plagiarism is the act of taking and using another's ideas and works and passing them off as one's own. This includes explicitly copying the whole work of another person and/or using some parts of their work without proper acknowledgement and referencing.

2. I hereby attest to the originality of this research proposal and has cited properly all the references used. I further commit that all deliverables and the final research study emanating from this proposal shall be of original content. I shall use appropriate citations in referring other work from various sources.

3. I understand that violation from this declaration and commitment shall be subject to consequences and shall be dealt with accordingly by the Department of Education.

**PROPONENT:**
PRINTED NAME:_______________
SIGNATURE:___________________
DATE : ___________________

## DECLARATION OF ABSENCE OF CONFLICT OF INTEREST

1. I, **(Name of the Researcher)** understand that conflict of interest refers to situations in which financial or other personal consideration may compromise may judgment in evaluating, conducting, or reporting research.

2. I hereby declare that we do not have any personal interest that may arise from the application and submission of my research proposal. I understand that my research proposal may be returned to me if found out that their conflict of interest during the initial screening as per DepEd Order No. 16, S, 2017

3. I understand that we may be held accountable by the Department of Education and for any conflict of interest which I have intentionally concealed.

**PROPONENT:**
PRINTED NAME: ________________
SIGNATURE: ________________
DATE : ________________

## Illustrative Example of Ethical Consideration

**Effectiveness of Claim, Evidence, and Reasoning as an Innovation to Develop Students' Scientific Argumentative Writing Skills (Samosa, 2021)**

**Ethical Consideration**

The researcher ensured that the identity of the respondents under study was kept anonymous to protect their reputations and dignity. This also entailed that the respondents are aware of the technicalities of the study and of their rights. Likewise, the study went through the right channels in obtaining permission from the institution first before the study is carried out.

## Types of Data Analyzed in Research

Once the data collected, they must be analyzed before adequate interpretation can be made. Through analysis, a researcher can do four things:

1. Describe the data clearly,
2. Identify what is typical or atypical among data,
3. Bring to light differences, relationship, and other patters existent in the data; and
4. Answer research question or test hypotheses.

While data analysis aims at the same general goals, qualitative and quantitative are analyze differently.

Qualitative data are analyzed inductively, a thought process that utilizes logic to make sense of observation in which.

1. Observations are made of behavior, situations, interaction, objects, and environments.
2. Topics are identified from the observation and are
3. Scrutinized to discover patterns and categories, then
4. Conclusions are deduced from what is observed and are stated verbally and finally.
5. Those conclusions are used to answer research questions.

Quantitative data, on the hand are analyzed mathematically and the results are expressed in statistical analysis is used to –

1. Depict what is typical among the data.
2. Show degrees of difference or relationship between two or more variables; and

3. Determine the likelihood that the findings are real for the population as opposed to having occurred only by chance in the sample.

## Methods of Analyzing Qualitative Data

Rebullida, et al. (1993), pointed out there are different ways of analyzing qualitative data. Some of these methods are as follows: comparative, institutional, descriptive, historical, inductive, deductive, content analysis and theory -based analysis.

1. **Comparative methods of analysis.** This method relies on comparison and contrast in the analysis of a phenomenon, object, or situation. In using this method, the researcher has to remember that the things to compared or contrasted have to belong to same category or class. Moreover, there has to be a basis for comparison and contrast.
2. **Institutional method of analysis.** This method examines the characteristics, behavior patterns, roles, structure, functions, and even development of established or observed institutions. Institutional method of analysis can be done using history, description, comparison, and contrast.
3. **Descriptive Methods of Analysis.** In this method of analysis, the researcher has to present in greater details the nature or characteristics of the phenomena or situation being described. Data analysis in this approach may take any of the following forms: establishing categories or typologies; and determining sequence of events or patterns of behavior.
4. **Historical Analysis.** This can be utilized when the researcher is after explaining events or phenomena in the past so as to understand the present. In this method of analysis, the researcher needs to trace the events which had taken place and, at the same time, come up with a meaningful way of comprehending and interpreting these events. Generalizations in historical analysis are arrived at, based on the patterns of events that the researcher is able to discover.
5. **Inductive Analysis.** This method of analyzing qualitative data allows the pattern of thinking and reasoning that starts from specific to universal. The process starts from particular observation and ends up with generalization based on these specific observations.
6. **Deductive analysis.** This is the exact opposite of the inductive method of analysis. Here, the researcher has to begin with a general statement about a phenomenon, situation, or object. He ends up by providing details, particular or specific facts to support the said general statement.
7. **Content analysis.** This method is appropriate to use when the researcher is concerned about explaining the status of some phenomenon at a particular time or its development over a period of time using available documents. Content analysis is also called documentary analysis. Sources of data for this method of analysis are as follows: records, reports, printed

forms, letters, autobiographies, diaries, compositions, themes or other academic works, books, periodicals, bulletins or catalogues, syllabi, court decisions, pictures, films, and cartoons.

## Methods of Analyzing Quantitative Data

Quantitative analysis is employed when the data to be analyzed are numerical or information which was assigned numerical values to facilitate counting, summarization, comparison, and generalization (Ardales, 1992). This type of analysis relies heavily on statistical techniques. Through statistics, the researcher can -

- Summarize data and reveal what is typical and atypical within a group.
- Show relative standing of individual in a group using percentile rankings, grade equivalents, age equivalents, and stanines;
- Show relationship among variables by means of statistical correlations;
- Show similarities and differences among groups with the use of the tests of differences;
- Identify error that is inherent in the selection of samples;
- Test for significance of findings; and
- Make other inferences about the population.

### Analytic Procedures for Quantitative Data.

There are five types of analytic procedure that a researcher can choose from, to answer the problems posed in his study namely: descriptive analysis, univariate analysis, bivariate analysis, multivariate analysis, and comparative analysis. Let us describe how each of these analytic procedures is done.

1. **Descriptive Analysis**. In this type of analysis, the researcher is only after describing the characteristics of the subjects under study. Data are usually analyzed to -
    - Identify the general characteristics of a group, with the use of descriptive statistics such as percentage, mean, median, and mode.
    - Determine differences in the group or how members of a group vary with reference to a given variable or factor being studied with the use of the standard deviation and coefficient of variation.

2. **Univariate analysis**. This type of analysis is employed when the researcher wants to analyze one variable or factor at a time. Univariate analysis relies heavily on the use of summary statistics, namely: measure of central tendency and measures if variability.

- **Mean** is the most common average used to indicate the most typical response. It is computed by dividing the sum of the values by the number of values or cases. It can only be subjected to arithmetical operations.
- **Median** is the middlemost value in an array, such that 50% are below it and 50% are above it. This is the appropriate average to use when the data are ordinal.
- **Mode** is the category or value with the greatest frequency of cases. It is the only acceptable indicator of the most typical case for data which are nominal or categorical.

Measures of variability are measures that reflect the amount of variation in the scores of a distribution. The most used measures for Univariate analysis are defined below.

- **Minimum and maximum values**. The minimum value indicates how far the spread toward the lower direction and the maximum value shows the extent of spread towards the upper direction from the average. These values describe the respondents or cases that represent the least and the most in whatever dimension is being measured.
- **Range**. It is simply the distance or difference between the maximum and minimum value, showing the total spread between extremes. It is the most unreliable measure of variability or dispersion as it is affected by extreme scores at either end of the distribution.
- **Standard deviation.** It is a measure of deviation or spread away from the mean. It is a single value that indicates the amount of dispersion in an array of scores.
- **Quartile deviation.** It is the appropriate measure of variability to employ when the median is the average used in describing a given distribution.

3. **Bivariate Analysis**. This type of analysis is used when the researcher is interested in probing into the relationship of two variables at a time. Bivariate analysis of relationship requires the use of Correlational statistics, such as Pearson's r, Spearman rho, Chi -square and other associational techniques.
4. **Multivariate Analysis**. This procedure for analyzing data is utilized when there is research question which cannot be responded using bivariate analysis. This analytic procedure permits the determination of the degree of relationship between one dependent variable and two or more independent variables simultaneously. The most used statistical tools for multivariate analysis are multiple regression analysis and multiple classification analysis.

5. **Comparative analysis.** When research participants must be compared based on certain variables being studied, comparative analysis is appropriate to use. This type of analysis requires the use of statistical tests of significant difference, like the t- test, critical ratio test and analysis of variance (ANOVA).

## Illustrative Example of Data Analysis

**CoSIM (Comics cum SIM): An Innovative Material in Teaching Biology (Samosa, 2021)**

**Data Analysis**

In analyzing the data, descriptive and inferential statistics will be employed. mean used to determine the average performance of pre-posttest and attitude test. The t-test will be employed to determine if there is a significant difference between the pretest-posttest before and after the implementation of CoSIM (Comics cum SIM) as an innovative material in teaching photosynthesis. More so, Pearson – product moment correlation coefficient was used to indicate the significant relationship of the respondent's academic performance and the level of academic performance and the attitudes towards exposure to CoSIM.

## Thematic Analysis for Qualitative Data

Thematic analysis is a flexible data analysis plan that qualitative researchers use to generate themes from interview data. According to Braun & Clarke (2006), It is best thought of as an umbrella term for a set of approaches for analyzing qualitative data that share a focus on identifying themes (patterns of meaning) in qualitative data.
There are six phases of Thematic Analysis.

1. **Familiarization with the data.** This phase involves reading and re-reading the data, to become immersed and intimately familiar with its content.
2. **Coding**. This phase involves generating succinct labels (codes) that identify important features of the data that might be relevant to answering the research question. It involves coding the entire dataset, and after that, collating all the codes and all relevant data extracts, together for later stages of analysis.
3. **Generating initial themes.** This phase involves examining the codes and collated data to identify significant broader patterns of meaning (potential themes). It then involves collating data relevant to each

candidate theme, so that you can work with the data and review the viability of each candidate theme.

4. **Reviewing themes.** This phase involves checking the candidate themes against the dataset, to determine that they tell a convincing story of the data, and one that answers the research question. In this phase, themes are typically refined, which sometimes involves them being split, combined, or discarded. In this approach, themes are defined as pattern of shared meaning underpinned by a central concept or idea.
5. **Defining and naming themes**. This phase involves developing a detailed analysis of each theme, working out the scope and focus of each theme, determining the 'story' of each. It also involves deciding on an informative name for each theme.
6. **Writing up.** This final phase involves weaving together the analytic narrative and data extracts and contextualizing the analysis in relation to existing literature.

There are different ways Thematic Analysis can be approached – within our reflexive approach all variations are possible:

1. An **inductive** way – coding and theme development are directed by the content of the data.
2. A **deductive** way – coding and theme development are directed by existing concepts or ideas.
3. A **semantic** way – coding and theme development reflect the explicit content of the data.
4. A **latent** way – coding and theme development report concepts and assumptions underpinning the data.
5. A **(critical) realist** or essentialist way – focuses on reporting an assumed reality evident in the data.
6. A **constructionist** way – focuses on looking at how a certain reality is created by the data.

More inductive, semantic and (critical) realist approaches tend to cluster together, ditto more deductive, latent and constructionist ones. In reality, the separation is not always that rigid. What is vitally important is that your analysis is theoretically coherent and consistent.

## A 15-point checklist of criteria for good thematic analysis (Braun & Clarke, 2006):

| Process | Criteria |
|---|---|
| **Transcription** | 1. The data have been transcribed to an appropriate level of detail, and the transcripts have been checked against the tapes for 'accuracy' |
| | 2. Each data item has been given equal attention in the coding |

| | |
|---|---|
| Coding | process. |
| | 3. Themes have not been generated from a few vivid examples (an anecdotal approach), but instead the coding process has been thorough, inclusive, and comprehensive. |
| | 4. All relevant extracts for all each theme have been collated. |
| | 5. Themes have been checked against each other and back to the original data set |
| | 6. Themes are internally coherent, consistent, and distinctive. |
| Analysis | 7. Data have been analyzed / interpreted, made sense of / rather than just paraphrased or described. |
| | 8. Analysis and data match each other / the extracts illustrate the analytic claims. |
| | 9. Analysis tells a convincing and well-organized story about the data and topic. |
| | 10. A good balance between analytic narrative and illustrative extracts is provided. |
| Overall | 11. Enough time has been allocated to complete all phases of the analysis adequately, without rushing a phase or giving it a once-over-lightly |
| Written report | 12. The assumptions about, and specific approach to, thematic analysis is clearly explicated. |
| | 13. There is a good fit between what you claim you do, and what you show you have done / ie, described method and reported analysis are consistent. |
| | 14. The language and concepts used in the report are consistent with the epistemological position of the analysis. |
| | 15. The researcher is positioned as active in the research process; themes do not just 'emerge'. |

## Content Analysis for Qualitative Data.

Content analysis is a research tool used to determine the presence of certain words, themes, or concepts within some given qualitative data (i.e. text). Using content analysis, researchers can quantify and analyze the presence, meanings and relationships of such certain words, themes, or concepts. It is any technique for making inferences by systematically and objectively identifying special characteristics of messages.

## Uses of Content Analysis

1. Identify the intentions, focus or communication trends of an individual, group or institution.
2. Describe attitudinal and behavioral responses to communications.
3. Determine psychological or emotional state of persons or groups.
4. Reveal international differences in communication content.
5. Reveal patterns in communication content.
6. Pre-test and improve an intervention or survey prior to launch.
7. Analyze focus group interviews and open-ended questions to complement quantitative data.

## Types of Content Analysis

There are two general types of content analysis: conceptual analysis and relational analysis. Conceptual analysis determines the existence and frequency of concepts in a text. Relational analysis develops the conceptual analysis further by examining the relationships among concepts in a text. Each type of analysis may lead to different results, conclusions, interpretations and meanings.

## Conceptual Analysis

Typically, people think of conceptual analysis when they think of content analysis. In conceptual analysis, a concept is chosen for examination and the analysis involves quantifying and counting its presence. The main goal is to examine the occurrence of selected terms in the data. Terms may be explicit or implicit. Explicit terms are easy to identify. Coding of implicit terms is more complicated: you need to decide the level of implication and base judgments on subjectivity (issue for reliability and validity). Therefore, coding of implicit terms involves using a dictionary or contextual translation rules or both.

To begin a conceptual content analysis, first identify the research question and choose a sample or samples for analysis. Next, the text must be coded into manageable content categories. This is basically a process of selective reduction. By reducing the text to categories, the researcher can focus on and code for specific words or patterns that inform the research question.

## General steps for conducting a conceptual content analysis:

1. **Decide the level of analysis: word, word sense, phrase, sentence, themes**.
2. **Decide how many concepts to code for develop pre-defined or interactive set of categories or concepts**. Decide either: A. to allow flexibility to add categories through the coding process, or B. to stick with the pre-defined set of categories.

- Option A allows for the introduction and analysis of new and important material that could have significant implications to one's research question.
- Option B allows the researcher to stay focused and examine the data for specific concepts.

3. **Decide whether to code for existence or frequency of a concept. The decision changes the coding process**.
   - When coding for the existence of a concept, the researcher would count a concept only once if it appeared at least once in the data and no matter how many times it appeared.
   - When coding for the frequency of a concept, the researcher would count the number of times a concept appears in a text.
4. **Decide on how you will distinguish among concepts.**
   - Should text be coded exactly as they appear or coded as the same when they appear in different forms? For example, "dangerous" vs. "dangerousness". The point here is to create coding rules so that these word segments are transparently categorized in a logical fashion. The rules could make all of these word segments fall into the same category, or perhaps the rules can be formulated so that the researcher can distinguish these word segments into separate codes.
   - What level of implication is to be allowed? Words that imply the concept or words that explicitly state the concept? For example, "dangerous" vs. "the person is scary" vs. "that person could cause harm to me". These word segments may not merit separate categories, due the implicit meaning of "dangerous".
5. **Develop rules for coding your texts**. After decisions of steps 1-4 are complete, a researcher can begin developing rules for translation of text into codes. This will keep the coding process organized and consistent. The researcher can code for exactly what he/she wants to code. Validity of the coding process is ensured when the researcher is consistent and coherent in their codes, meaning that they follow their translation rules. In content analysis, obeying by the translation rules is equivalent to validity.
6. **Decide what to do with irrelevant information**. should this be ignored (e.g. common English words like "the" and "and"), or used to reexamine the coding scheme in the case that it would add to the outcome of coding?
7. **Code the text.** This can be done by hand or by using software. By using software, researchers can input categories and have coding done automatically, quickly and efficiently, by the software program. When coding is done by hand, a researcher can recognize error far more easily (e.g. typos, misspelling). If using computer coding, text could be

cleaned of errors to include all available data. This decision of hand vs. computer coding is most relevant for implicit information where category preparation is essential for accurate coding.

8. **Analyze your results.** Draw conclusions and generalizations where possible. Determine what to do with irrelevant, unwanted or unused text: reexamine, ignore, or reassess the coding scheme. Interpret results carefully as conceptual content analysis can only quantify the information. Typically, general trends and patterns can be identified.

## Relational Analysis

Relational analysis begins like conceptual analysis, where a concept is chosen for examination. However, the analysis involves exploring the relationships between concepts. Individual concepts are viewed as having no inherent meaning and rather the meaning is a product of the relationships among concepts.

To begin a relational content analysis, first identify a research question and choose a sample or samples for analysis. The research question must be focused so the concept types are not open to interpretation and can be summarized. Next, select text for analysis. Select text for analysis carefully by balancing having enough information for a thorough analysis so results are not limited with having information that is too extensive so that the coding process becomes too arduous and heavy to supply meaningful and worthwhile results.

There are three subcategories of relational analysis to choose from prior to going on to the general steps.

a) **Affect extraction**. an emotional evaluation of concepts explicit in a text. A challenge to this method is that emotions can vary across time, populations, and space. However, it could be effective at capturing the emotional and psychological state of the speaker or writer of the text.

b) **Proximity analysis**. an evaluation of the co-occurrence of explicit concepts in the text. Text is defined as a string of words called a "window" that is scanned for the co-occurrence of concepts. The result is the creation of a "concept matrix", or a group of interrelated co-occurring concepts that would suggest an overall meaning.

c) **Cognitive mapping**. a visualization technique for either affect extraction or proximity analysis. Cognitive mapping attempts to create a model of the overall meaning of the text such as a graphic map that represents the relationships between concepts.

**General steps for conducting a relational content analysis:**

1. **Determine the type of analysis**. Once the sample has been selected, the researcher needs to determine what types of relationships to examine and the level of analysis: word, word sense, phrase, sentence, themes.
2. **Reduce the text to categories and code for words or patterns**. A researcher can code for existence of meanings or words.
3. **Explore the relationship between concepts**. once the words are coded, the text can be analyzed for the following:
   - Strength of relationship: degree to which two or more concepts are related.
   - Sign of relationship: are concepts positively or negatively related to each other?
   - Direction of relationship: the types of relationship that categories exhibit. For example, "X implies Y" or "X occurs before Y" or "if X then Y" or if X is the primary motivator of Y.
4. **Code the relationships**. a difference between conceptual and relational analysis is that the statements or relationships between concepts are coded.
5. **Perform statistical analyses**. explore differences or look for relationships among the identified variables during coding.
6. **Map out representations**. such as decision mapping and mental models.

**Choosing the Appropriate Statistical Test and Techniques for Analyzing Quantitative Data.**

In statistics, for each of the specific situation, statistical methods are available for analysis and interpretation of the data. To select the appropriate statistical method, one need to know the assumption and conditions of the statistical methods, so that proper statistical method can be selected for data analysis. Two main statistical methods are used in data analysis: ***descriptive statistics***, which summarizes data using indexes such as mean and median and another is ***inferential statistics***, which draw conclusions from data using statistical tests such as student's *t*-test. **Selection of appropriate statistical method depends on the following three things**:

1. **Aim and objective of the study**. Selection of statistical test depends upon our aim and objective of the study. Suppose our objective is to find out the predictors of the outcome variable, then regression analysis is used while to compare the means between two independent samples, unpaired samples t-test is used.
2. **Type and distribution of the data used**. For the same objective, selection of the statistical test is varying as per data types. For the

nominal, ordinal, discrete data, we use nonparametric methods while for continuous data, parametric methods as well as nonparametric methods are used. For example, in the regression analysis, when our outcome variable is categorical, logistic regression while for the continuous variable, linear regression model is used. The choice of the most appropriate representative measure for continuous variable is dependent on how the values are distributed. If continuous variable follows normal distribution, mean is the representative measure while for non-normal data, median is considered as the most appropriate representative measure of the data set. Similarly, in the categorical data, proportion (percentage) while for the ranking/ordinal data, mean ranks are our representative measure. In the inferential statistics, hypothesis is constructed using these measures and further in the hypothesis testing, these measures are used to compare between/among the groups to calculate significance level.

3. **Nature of the observations (paired/unpaired).** Another important point in selection of the statistical test is to assess whether data is paired (same subjects are measures at different time points or using different methods) or unpaired (each group have different subject). For example, to compare the means between two groups, when data is paired, paired samples t-test while for unpaired (independent) data, independent samples t-test is used.

## Concept of Parametric and Nonparametric Methods

Inferential statistical methods fall into two possible categorizations: parametric and nonparametric. All type of statistical methods those are used to compare the means are called parametric while statistical methods used to compare other than means (ex-median/mean ranks/proportions) are called ***nonparametric methods***. ***Parametric tests*** rely on the assumption that the variable is continuous and follow approximate normally distributed. When data is continuous with non-normal distribution or any other types of data other than continuous variable, nonparametric methods are used. Fortunately, the most frequently used parametric methods have nonparametric counterparts. This can be useful when the assumptions of a parametric test are violated, and researcher can choose the nonparametric alternative as a backup analysis.

**Parametric tests**

1. **Mean** - The mean is more commonly called the average; however, this is incorrect if "mean" is taken in the specific sense of "arithmetic mean" as there are different types of averages: the mean, median, and mode.
2. **Standard Deviation** - The standard deviation measures the spread of the data about the mean value. It is useful in comparing sets of data, which may have the same mean but a different range.
3. **t test** - The t-test assesses whether the means of two groups are statistically different from each other. This analysis is appropriate whenever you want to compare the means of two group.
4. **Analysis of variance (ANOVA)** – This is used to test hypotheses about differences between two or more means as in the t-test, however when there are more than two means, analysis of variance can be used to test differences for significance without increasing the error rate (Type I).
5. **Pearson correlation** – This is a common measure of the correlation between two variables. A correlation of +1 means that there is a perfect positive linear relationship between variables. A correlation of -1 means that there is a perfect negative linear relationship between variables.
6. **Regression (linear and nonlinear)** - A technique used for the modelling and analysis of numerical data. Regression can be used for prediction (including forecasting of time-series data), inference, hypothesis testing, and modelling of causal relationships.

**Non-parametric tests**

1. **Median -** The median is the middle of a distribution: half the scores are above the median and half are below the median. The median is less sensitive to extreme scores than the mean and this makes it a better measure than the mean for highly skewed distributions. The median income is usually more informative than the mean income for example.
2. **Interquartile range -** The interquartile range (IQR) is the distance between the 75th percentile and the 25th percentile. The IQR is essentially the range of the middle 50% of the data. Because it uses the middle 50%, the IQR is not affected by outliers or extreme values.
3. **Spearman correlation -** Spearman's Rank Correlation is a technique used to test the direction and strength of the relationship between two variables. In other words, it's a device to show whether any one set of numbers has an effect on another set of numbers.
4. **Chi - square test.** It is used as an inferential statistic for nominal or categorical data. This is the most versatile among the test of statistical significance, as can be both as a test of relationship or test of difference. When employed as a test of relationship, it is called a test of

independence. When used as a test of difference, it is considered a test of homogeneity.

5. **Wilcoxon test -** The Wilcoxon test compares two paired groups of data. It calculates the differences between each set of pairs and analyses the list of differences.
6. **Mann-Whitney test** – it is a non-parametric test for assessing whether two samples of observations come from the same distribution, testing the null hypothesis that the probability of an observation from one population exceeds the probability of an observation in a second population.
7. **Kruskal-Wallis test -** A non-parametric method for testing equality of population medians among groups, using a one-way analysis of variance by ranks.
8. **Friedman test -** it is a nonparametric test that compares three or more paired groups.

**Parametric and their Alternative Nonparametric Methods**

| Description | Parametric Methods | Nonparametric Methods |
|---|---|---|
| **Descriptive statistics** | Mean, Standard deviation | Median, Interquartile range |
| **Sample with population (or hypothetical value)** | One sample *t*-test ($n$ <30) and One sample *Z*-test ($n$ ≥30) | One sample Wilcoxon signed rank test |
| **Two unpaired groups** | Independent samples *t*-test (Unpaired samples *t*-test) | Mann Whitney U test/Wilcoxon rank sum test |
| **Two paired groups** | Paired samples *t*-test | Related samples Wilcoxon signed-rank test |
| **Three or more unpaired groups** | One-way ANOVA | Kruskal-Wallis H test |
| **Degree of linear relationship** | Pearson's correlation coefficient | Spearman rank correlation coefficient |
| **Predict one outcome variable by at least one independent variable** | Linear regression model | Nonlinear regression model/Log linear regression model on log normal data. |

## Statistical Methods to Compare the Proportions

The statistical methods used to compare the proportions are considered nonparametric methods and these methods have no alternative parametric methods.

**Pearson Chi-square test and Fisher exact test** is used to compare the proportions between two or more independent groups.

To test the change in proportions between two paired groups, **McNemar test** is used while **Cochran Q test** is used for the same objective among three or more paired groups.

**Z test** for proportions is used to compare the proportions between two groups for independent as well as dependent groups.

**Statistical Methods to Compare the Proportions**

| Description | Statistical Methods | Data Type |
|---|---|---|
| **Test the association between two categorical variables (Independent groups)** | Pearson Chi-square test/Fisher exact test | Variable has ≥2 categories |
| **Test the change in proportions between 2/3 groups (paired groups)** | McNemar test/Cochrane Q test | Variable has 2 categories |
| **Comparisons between proportions** | Z test for proportions | Variable has 2 categories |

**Summarizes the four levels of measurement scales and the appropriate statistics for each level.**

| Scales of measurement | Relations being defined | Appropriate statistical test to be used | Examples of statistical that can be used. |
|---|---|---|---|
| **Nominal** | Equivalence | Nonparametric test | Mode, frequency, Chi-square test |
| **Ordinal** | Equivalence, greater than, less than | Nonparametric test | Median, Spearman rank, Friedman's test, Kendall's tau percentile |
| **Interval** | Equivalence, greater than, less than, known ratio of any two | Nonparametric and parametric test | Mean, standard deviation, z -test, t-test, ANOVA, |

| | intervals | | Pearson's r |
|---|---|---|---|
| **Ratio** | Equivalence, greater than, less than, known ratio of any two ratio | Nonparametric and parametric test | Mean, standard deviation, coefficient of variation, z -test, t-test, ANOVA, Pearson's r |

Quantitative variables like nominal and ordinal variables cannot make use of parametric statistical test unlike interval and ratio variables. Interval and ratio levels of measurement can be applied with both the parametric and nonparametric statistical tests. In parametric statistical tests, we can conveniently make use of the mean and standard deviation, the z- test, the t-test, the analysis of variance (ANOVA), and the Chi - square test, the Friedman's test, Kendall's tau, the Binomial test, the Spearman rank correlation, the Kruskall - Wallis test, and Wilcoxon signed rank test, to name a few, to interval and ratio levels of measurements. Interval and ratio measurement can be reduced to nominal or ordinal measurement, while nominal and ordinal measures cannot be upgraded to interval or ratio measures.

## Graphic Representation of Data

Graphic representation is another way of analyzing numerical data. A graph is a sort of chart through which statistical data are represented in the form of lines or curves drawn across the coordinated points plotted on its surface. Graphs enable the researcher to study the cause-and-effect relationship between two variables. Graphs help to measure the extent of change in one variable when another variable changes by a certain amount. Graphs also enable us in studying both time series and frequency distribution as they give clear account and precise picture of problem.

## Methods to Represent a Frequency Distribution

Generally, four methods are used to represent a frequency distribution graphically. These are Histogram, Smoothed frequency graph and Ogive or Cumulative frequency graph and pie diagram.

1. **Histogram** is a non-cumulative frequency graph; it is drawn on a natural scale in which the representative frequencies of the different class of values are represented through vertical rectangles drawn closed to each other. Measure of central tendency, mode can be easily determined with the help of this graph. **Frequency Polygon** it is a frequency graph which is drawn

by joining the coordinating points of the mid-values of the class intervals and their corresponding frequencies.

2. **Smoothed Frequency Polygon.** When the sample is very small, and the frequency distribution is irregular the polygon is very jig-jag. In order to wipe out the irregularities and "also get a better notion of how the figure might look if the data were more numerous, the frequency polygon may be smoothed." In this process to adjust the frequencies we take a series of 'moving' or 'running' averages. To get an adjusted or smoothed frequency we add the frequency of a class interval with the two adjacent intervals, just below and above the class interval. Then the sum is divided by 3. When these adjusted frequencies are plotted against the class intervals on a graph it refers to a smoothed frequency polygon.
3. **Ogive or Cumulative Frequency Polygon.** Ogive is a cumulative frequency graphs drawn on natural scale to determine the values of certain factors like median, Quartile, Percentile etc. In these graphs the exact limits of the class intervals are shown along the X-axis and the cumulative frequen-cies are shown along the Y-axis. Below are given the steps to draw an ogive.
4. **Pie Diagram.** it is a circular statistical graphic, which is divided into slices to illustrate numerical proportion. it is useful when one wants to picture proportions of the total in a striking way. When a population is stratified and each stratum is to be presented as a percentage at that time pie diagram is used.

### Illustrative Example of Results and Discussion

**CoSIM (Comics cum SIM): An Innovative Material in Teaching Biology (Samosa, 2021)**

**Results and Discussion**

This part present both tabular and textual manner the data gathered from the results of the attitude survey and pretest-posttest of students. The data were treated with appropriate statistical test and were analyzed and interpreted to determine the answers to the questions posed in the study.

**Table 2. The students' academic performance before and after the utilization of CoSIM.**

| | Pretest | Posttest | Gain Score |
|---|---|---|---|
| **Mean** | 19.20 | 36.43 | 17.23 |

Looking at the Table 2, were the students' academic performance before and after the utilization of CoSIM. Taking into account the data provided on the table, it indicates that before the utilization of CoSIM students' academic performance in pretest were 19.20, then in posttest were 36.43. Hence, the students' gain the score of 17.23. More so, it can be concluded that CoSIM had a positive effect on the performance of the students, as evidenced by the significantly greater mean in the posttest than in the pretest. The study confirmed the finding of Anderson et al. (2012) Salviejo et al (2014), Barredo (2014), Dapitan & Caballes (2019), Sinco (2020), that utilization strategic intervention materials in the least-learned competencies in biology improved the students' academic performance. More so, the study supported the findings of Hosler & Boomer, (2012), Da Silva et. al (2016), Casumpang & Enteria (2019), that comics was effective as an instructional material in teaching science concepts.

**Table 3. The level of students' attitude in the utilization of CoSIM**

| | Mean Score | Interpretation |
|---|---|---|
| **Attitude** | 4.75 | **High Positive Attitude** |

The Table 3 established the level of students' attitude in the utilization of CoSIM. Looking forward, the data presented on the table showed that students have high positive attitude in learning biology concepts in photosynthesis based on the mean score 4.75, it indicates that utilization of CoSIM, the students has enjoyed, appreciated, and interested in learning concepts as exposed to intervention materials. It further agrees with different assertions coming from different existing studies of Hosler & Boomer (2012), Affeldt et al. (2018), and Casumpang & Enteria (2019), comics was effective as an instructional material in promoting positive learning attitude towards science concepts.

**Table 4: T-test for pretest and posttest score of students in the utilization of CoSIM**

| t- test computed value | df | t-test critical value | Probability Level | Decision | Interpretation |
|---|---|---|---|---|---|
| 16.89 | 29 | 2.048 | $< 0.05$ | **$H_o$ is rejected** | **Significant** |

Upon computing the data, it appeared that the t- value is 16.89 was exceeds in the t- critical value of 2.048 at the degree of freedom of 29. The result is significant at $p < 0.05$. Therefore, the null hypothesis is thereby, rejected. Thus, there is significant difference in the pretest and posttest score of students in the utilization of CoSIM. The claim is also supported with the study of Arroio (2011) and Weber, et al. (2013) stating that the use of visual and text format presentation gives comic a potential in getting away from traditional mode of delivering classes with the use of traditional textbook materials.

**Table 5: Test of Relationship between students' academic performance and students' attitude in the utilization of CoSIM**

| Pearson r | Relationship | Degree of freedom | t- test computed value | t-test critical value | Probability Level | Decision | Interpretation |
|---|---|---|---|---|---|---|---|
| .76 | High relationship | 28 | 6.06 | 2.048 | < 0.05 | **$H_o$ is rejected** | **Significant** |

The data revealed the obtained pearson r value is .76 which denotes high positive relationship. This means the higher the academic performance, the higher is the level of students' attitude toward utilization of CoSIM. Since the t-value, 6.06 is greater than the t- critical value, 2.048 at 0.05 and degree of freedom of 28, giving the researcher reasons to reject the null hypothesis in favor of researcher hypothesis. This may be safely concluded that students' academic performance significantly related to the students' attitude toward the utilization of CoSIM in teaching biology particularly in the concepts of photosynthesis.

## Reporting Findings, Drawing Conclusions and Making Recommendations

After the collection of data and collating, presenting, analyzing, interpreting, and discussing the results, the formulation of concluding part of the research follows. The concluding part is composed of the summary of finding, conclusion, and recommendation.

### Summary of Findings.

The summary of findings puts together the highlight of the important findings of the study. It is a condensation of the steps taken by the researcher and the subsequent findings. In a very concise manner, the researcher restates the problems, the methods used, techniques and tools utilized in gathering and interpreting the data and then, states the answers to the action research questions.

In summarizing the findings of the study, specific problems are restated one at a time and these followed by the highlight of the results of the investigation. The summary of findings serves as an overview or a resume of the most important findings of the entire inquiry.

If there are only two specific answers or findings in sections, there should only two results/findings summarized in this section. Tables, graph and other figures of presentation are excluded here. Important results are stated as concisely and as directly as possible.

Ariola (2006), suggested the following guidelines in writing summary of findings.

1. Enumeration of findings should follow the sequence of the subproblems of the study.
2. Only important major findings should be highlighted.
3. Findings should be stated as cautiously as possible without further discussion.
4. The findings must be consistent with the analysis of data.
5. No new data should be introduced into the findings if they are not found in the analysis of data, or not part of the study.

## Conclusions

The conclusion (s) is an abstraction drawn from the findings of the study and is tied to the questions investigated. Conclusion should be consistent with and must drawn from the findings. If there are only two summarized results, there must also be conclusions. Conclusions should be arranged in accordance with the presentation and arrangement of the findings. Rejection or acceptance of the hypothesis (es) are explained briefly in this section. Conclusion should be stated briefly and in straight forward manner so that reader can remember it easily, it is important that every problem raised, a conclusion is reached by the researcher.

The following guidelines in writing conclusions.

1. Conclusions are inferences, deductions, abstractions, implications, interpretation, general statements, and or generalizations based upon the findings. Conclusions are the logical and valid outgrowth of the findings. They should not contain any numerals because numerals generally limit the forceful effect or impact and scope of the generalization. No conclusion be made that are not based upon the findings.
2. Conclusions should appropriately answer the specific questions raised at the beginning of the investigation in the order they are given under the statement of the problem. The study becomes almost meaningless if the questions raised are not properly answered by the conclusions.
3. Conclusion should point out what were factually learned from the inquiry. However, no conclusion should be drawn from the implied or indirect effects of the findings.
4. Conclusions should be formulated concisely, that is, brief and short, yet the convey all the necessary information resulting from the study as required by the specific questions.
5. Without any strong evidence to the contrary, conclusion should be stated categorically. They should be worded as if they are 100 percent true and correct. They should not give any hint that the researchers have some doubts about their validity and reliability. The

use of qualifiers such as probably, perhaps, may be and the like should be avoided as much as possible.

6. Conclusions should refer only to the population, area, or subject of the study.
7. Conclusions should not be repetitions of any statements anywhere in the thesis. They may be recapitulations if necessary, but they should be worded differently, and they should convey the same information as the statement recapitulated.

## Recommendations

Recommendation are suggestions for the improvement of the existing policies, practices, program or prevailing conditions under study. The main goal of research is the betterment and or improvement of life and this goal should be the focal point in writing the recommendations.

Recommendations should be derived from the data gathered and from the conclusion drawn from the findings. Its common practice to enumerate the recommendations and number them and to identify specific person, institutions, or sections to whom the recommendations are addressed.

The following guidelines in writing recommendations.

1. Make sure that your recommendations are in accordance with the conclusion and limitation of your study. Furthermore, align your recommendation with the purpose and scope of your research.
2. Make your recommendation as specific as possible for them to become workable and practical.
3. Write your recommendations concisely and clearly. This will help the readers immediately recognize the impact of your study.
4. As much as possible, refrain from offering recommendations that could have been easily addressed as you were conducting your study. Otherwise, these might be construed only as an after -thought.

## Illustrative Examples of Conclusions and Recommendations

**Effectiveness of Claim, Evidence, and Reasoning as an Innovation to Develop Students' Scientific Argumentative Writing Skills (Samosa, 2021)**

**Conclusions**

The research results of and discussion on the effectiveness of CER as innovation to develop students' scientific argumentative writing skills in Biology teaching draw several conclusions.

1. The students' scientific argumentative writing skills in biology learning after the CER framework application is found at the proficient in writing the claim, proficient in writing evidence and excelling in writing the reasoning. This research has implied that CER as innovation are effectively increased the components of writing the claim, evidence, and reasoning in biology teaching.
2. The students have high positive attitude based on the five indicators toward nature of science after the CER framework application.
3. After the CER framework application, the students improved their appreciation in learning of science into positive attitude.
4. It is evident that after the CER, students' appreciation in scientific writing improved into positive attitude.
5. The students have high positive attitude based on the five indicators toward thinking and learning science after the CER framework application.
6. After the students are very comfortable in using CER as innovation to develop students' scientific argumentative writing skills.
7. The implementation of CER results is the significant improvement on students' scientific argumentative writing skills in biology teaching after the experiment
8. Claim, Evidence and Reasoning increases students' ability to identify, critique, and compare the quality of evidence in written arguments.
9. Participation in argumentative writing exercises helps to strengthen Students' scientific claims.
10. Students need continuous feedback in order to improve and to think-like- a scientist.

**Recommendations.**

Based on the findings of the study and the conclusion drawn, the following are recommended:

1. Further research is needed on possible connections between argumentative writing instruction in the science curriculum and the language arts curriculum, and how teachers can potentially collaborate and/or design curriculum to support this practice among the different content areas.
2. Utilize the used of the CER Framework in teaching science subjects for further research with bigger population.
3. Conduct a School – Based workshop on proper implementation of the CER as innovation to develop students' scientific argumentative writing skills.
4. For more comprehensive findings, further studies on the same area of concentration may be conducted for improving science education where the students will be benefited.

**List the References.**

The reference list complies all the bibliographic information for the materials you used in preparing your research. Providing a reference list aids your readers in tracing the works that guided you in conducting your study, thus making your research more reliable. It also helps you avoid committing intellectual dishonesty since a reference list is proof that you acknowledge other studies that shapes your own.

Below are some guidelines you can follow in listing your references

1. **Make sure that your reference list contains all of the works and publication you used for your research**. All the references that you cited in the text itself must be included in your reference list.
2. **Cite your sources completely**. Aside from providing the name of the references itself, you need to cite the author of the work; the publisher of the material (if it is printed); the date of its publication or release; and the date that you retrieved it (if it is an online reference).
3. **Exercise consistency in the format of your bibliographical entries**. Strictly follow the format for citing your references according to the citation style you are using in your research (APA, MLA, or Chicago). The citation style you are using will also determine the title or heading of your reference list. Paper written in the APA style use heading "Reference", the MLA Style uses the heading "Works Cited," and the Chicago style uses the heading "Bibliography."
4. **Take note of other consideration in citing your references.** For instance, make sure to arrange your references alphabetically. In addition, use en dash (–) instead of hyphen (-) when presenting range (e.g., 5 – 13)

**7th Editions of the APA Referencing Style.**

1. **The publisher location is no longer included in reference list entries.**

   **APA 6th Edition**

   Samosa, R.C (2021). Understanding the End- to -End Praxis of Quantitative Research: From Scratch to Paper Presentation. Las Pinas City, Philippines: Book of Life Publishing.

   **APA 7th Edition**

   Samosa, R.C (2021). Understanding the End- to -End Praxis of Quantitative Research: From Scratch to Paper Presentation. Book of Life Publishing.
2. **In-text citation for works with three or more authors has been shortened. From the very first citation, only include the first author's name and "et al."**

**APA 6th Edition**

(Samosa, Capulso, Baustista, Carlos, & Dela Cruz, 2020).

**APA 7th Edition**

(Samosa et al., 2020).

3. **Surnames and initials for up to 20 authors (instead of 7) should be provided in the reference list.**

**APA 6th Edition**

Lenes, E., Swank, J., Hart, K., Machado, M., Darilus, S., Ardelt, M., … Puig, A. (2020). Color-conscious multicultural mindfulness training in the counseling field. Journal of Counseling & Development, 98(2), 147–158. https://doi.org/10.1002/jcad.12309.

**APA 7th Edition**

Lenes, E., Swank, J., Hart, K., Machado, M., Darilus, S., Ardelt, M., Smith-Adcock, S., Rockwood, L., & Puig, A. (2020). Color-conscious multicultural mindfulness training in the counseling field. Journal of Counseling & Development, 98(2), 147–158. https://doi.org/10.1002/jcad.12309

4. **DOIs are formatted the same as URLs. They should begin with https and the label 'DOI:' is no longer necessary.**

**APA 6th Edition**

Daltry, R. (2020). Embedded therapy dog: Bringing a therapy dog into your counseling center. Journal of College Student Psychotherapy, 34(2), 118–124. DOI:10.1080/87568225.2018.1544841

**APA 7th Edition**

Daltry, R. (2020). Embedded therapy dog: Bringing a therapy dog into your counseling center. Journal of College Student Psychotherapy, 34(2), 118–124. https://doi.org/10.1080/87568225.2018.1544841

***Always use the doi if available whether the source is in print or accessible online***

5. URLs are no longer preceded by 'Retrieved from' unless a retrieval date is needed. The website name is included (unless it's the same as the author), and all web page titles are italicised.

**APA 6th Edition**

Keen, L. (2019, October 25). LGBTQI Indigenous young people urged to be true to who they are. Retrieved from https://www.abc.net.au/news/2019-10-25/black-proud-out-and-loud-a-community-comes-together/11632608

**APA 7th Edition**

Keen, L. (2019, October 25). *LGBTQI Indigenous young people urged to be true to who they are. ABC News.*

https://www.abc.net.au/news/2019-10-25/black-proud-out-and-loud-a-community-comes-together/11632608

6. For ebooks and articles, the format, platform, or device (e.g. Kindle) and 'Retrieved from' statements are no longer included in the reference. For ebooks, the publisher is now included.

   **APA 6th Edition**

   Bush, S. S., Connell, M. A., & Denney, R. L. (2019). Ethical practice in forensic psychology: A guide for mental health professionals [Kindle version]. Retrieved from https://ebookcentral.proquest.com

   **APA 7th Edition**

   Bush, S. S., Connell, M. A., & Denney, R. L. (2019). Ethical practice in forensic psychology: A guide for mental health professionals. American Psychological Association.

***If a DOI is available always add it to the end of the reference entry.***

**Action Research Work Plan and Timeliness**

You are done with the details of your action research plan. All you need to do now is to prepare a simplified guide for you to follow. Remember that action research aims to address an urgent classroom problem. It is therefore imperative that you conduct the study as scheduled. This will make your study responsive to your emerging problem.

In this part you will list down all activities relative to your research with the corresponding timeline. Specify the start and the end target dates. This will help you keep track of the progress of your research undertaking. Should you wish to present the timeline through the Gantt Chart, you may do so. Individual who will be involved in your study should be pre-identified. This will give you an idea as to who could possibly assist you in every step of your research.

| Objectives | Activity | Time Allotment | Person Involve | Resources (Budget) | Expected Output | Accomplishment | Actual Accomplishment (Remarks) |
|---|---|---|---|---|---|---|---|
| Pre- Implementation | | | | | | | |
| 1. | | | | | | | |
| 2. | | | | | | | |
| 3. | | | | | | | |
| Implementation | | | | | | | |
| 1. | | | | | | | |
| 2. | | | | | | | |
| 3. | | | | | | | |
| Post -Implementation | | | | | | | |
| 1. | | | | | | | |
| 2. | | | | | | | |
| 3. | | | | | | | |

## WORK PLAN

| OBJECTIVES | ACTIVITY | TIME ALLOTMENT | PERSON/S INVOLVED | RESOURCE/ BUDGET | EXPECTED OUTPUT/TARGET | ACCOMPLISHMENT | ACTUAL ACCOMPLISHMENT & REMARKS |
|---|---|---|---|---|---|---|---|
| **A. PRE-IMPLEMENTATION PHASE** | | | | | | | |
| 1. Present the proposal to the School Management | Formal presentation through consultation or institutional colloquium | July 1,2019 | Researcher and Principal | Paper | 100% approved by the management | Approved letter of endorsement | |
| 2. Accomplish preliminary part of the research (Chapter 1-3) | Writeshop | July 1-27, 2019 | Researcher | Bond paper, computer, printer | 100% accomplished preliminary part of research | Accomplished preliminary part of the research paper | |
| 3. Diagnose students' understanding on bioenergetics | Conducting Pretest | July 29, 2019 | Researcher | Pretest 100 reproduction of test and answer sheets | 100% accomplished in conducting pretest among pupils | Documents of pretest answered test papers. | |
| 4. Craft lesson plan in teaching bioenergetics using Claim-Evidence - Reasoning framework. | Lesson Planning | July 30 - August 9, 2019 | Researcher | Lesson Plan | 100% done with the lesson plan | Crafted lesson plan | |
| 5. Prepare materials intended for the lesson | Material preparation | August 12 - 23, 2019 | Researcher | Materials: Laboratory Worksheet, Laboratory Equipment, Projector, Laptop. | 100% done with the needed instructional materials for the lesson | Needed instructional materials for the lesson | |
| **B. IMPLEMENTATION PHASE** | | | | | | | |
| 1. Present the lesson using Claim- Evidence - Reasoning framework. | Instructional delivery and conducting Claim- Evidence - Reasoning framework. | August 26 -September 6, 2019 | Researcher and Students | Prepared materials | 100% accomplished lesson delivery for research purpose | Documentation | |
| 2. Documentation the discussion using the mentioned framework | Assign students to take pictures of the activity as part of the latter's portfolio | August 26 -September 6, 2019 | Researcher and Students | Mobile Phone for documentation, clearbook, printing cost, bondpaper. | 100% collection of pictures and collage of documentations done | Documentation | |

| OBJECTIVES | ACTIVITY | TIME ALLOTMENT | PERSON/S INVOLVED | RESOURCE/ BUDGET | EXPECTED OUTPUT/TARGET | ACCOMPLISHMENT | ACTUAL ACCOMPLISHMENT & REMARKS |
|---|---|---|---|---|---|---|---|
| 3. Assess the effects of Claim-Evidence – Reasoning framework on student scientific argumentation writing skills through posttest | Conducting Post test | September 9 ,2019 | Researcher | Post test Copies of answer sheets | 100% conducted post test among students | Documentation and answered test papers | |
| 4. Record and analyze the test results | Recording and analysis of data | September 10-12, 2019 | Researcher | Papers, computer using SPSS | 100% recording and result analysis completed | Report paper on analyzed results | |
| **C. POST -IMPLEMENTATION PHASE** | | | | | | | |
| 1. Present the result of post test | Result presentation through consultation | September 13,2019 | Researcher and Principal | Data | 100% accomplished presenting the result of post test | Documentation minutes of the meeting certificate of presentation | |
| 2. Tally and compute the data using intended statistical tools | Statistical computation and coding of the interviews | September 16-20, 2019 | Researcher | Data, Computer | 100% completed the tallying and computation of data | Report on tallied data. | |
| 3. Prepare the remaining parts of paper for completions | Writeshop | September 23-30, 2019 | Researcher | Bondpaper, printer | 100% accomplished in completing the paper | Whole paper | |
| 4. Review entirely the work and submit for critiquing and evaluation | Paper review and critiquing | November 3-29,2019 | Researcher, Principal, colleagues, graduate school professors, division supervisors. | Completed paper | Submitted the paper for critiquing and evaluation | Paper draft with corrections and comments | |
| 5. Finalize the paper and ensure the complete parts | Preparation and submission completed of paper | December 10, 2019 | Researcher | Completed paper | 100% done with the paper upon evaluated | Completed paper | Fully Accomplished |
| 6. Present paper for conference | Paper presentation | December 16, 2019 January 10, 2020 | Researcher | Full paper, registration fees, accommodation, transportation. | Presented paper in the conference | Certificate of presentation, documentation, program of proceedings | Fully Accomplished |
| 7. Present results to co-teachers and share findings | Research dissemination | Within the School Year | Researcher & teachers | Research paper | Research presentation done with teachers | Documentation, minutes the meeting, certification | Fully Accomplished |

**Prepared by:**

RESTY C. SAMOSA

RESEARCHER

**Checked by:**

RESTY C. SAMOSA

RESEARCH COORDINATOR

**Approved by:**

MARIETTA G. LICOPIT

PRINCIPAL I

**Cost Estimates**

As a classroom teacher who desires to improve performance, to conduct an action research is a milestone. However, an action research just like any project entails resources. For you to have an estimate of the possible expenses you would need in the entire research process, you may use this template. Include all activities with corresponding monetary requirements relative to your research.

As stated in DepEd Order No. 16, s. 2017, school- based action research may be granted Basic Education Research Fund (BERF) of not more than ₱ 30,000.00. You may also opt to look for benefactors or entities who could help you in your research study aside from BERF.

| Activities | Resources Needed | Amount |
|---|---|---|
| **Pre- Implementation** | | |
| 1. | | |
| 2. | | |
| **Implementation** | | |
| 1. | | |
| 2. | | |
| **Post- Implementation** | | |
| 1. | | |
| 2. | | |
| **Total Amount** | | |

**Plans for Dissemination and Utilization**

While the ultimate goal of your research is to promote effective change in your classroom or schools, do not underestimate the value of sharing your findings with others. Sharing your results helps you further reflect on the process and problem, and it allows others to use your results to helps them in their own endeavors to improve the education of their students.

You can report your findings in many different ways. You most certainly will want to share the experience with your students, parents, teachers, and principal. Provide them with an overview of the process and share highlights from your research journal. Since each of these audiences is different, you will need to adjust the content and delivery of the information each time you share. You may also want to present your process at conference so educators from other district can benefits from your work.

As your skill with the action research cycle becomes more refined, you may want to develop an abstract and submit an article to an educational journal. To write an abstract, state the problem you were trying to solve, describe your context, details your action plan and methods, summarize your findings, state your conclusions and explain your revised action plan.

The reporting of action research most often occurs in informal settings that are far less intimidating than the venues where scholarly research has traditionally been shared. Faculty meetings, seminars, and teacher conferences are among the most common venues for sharing action research with peers. However, each year more and more teacher researchers are writing up their work for publication or to help fulfill requirements in graduate programs. Regardless of which venue or techniques you select for reporting on research, the simple knowledge that you are contributing to a collective knowledge regarding teaching and learning proves to be among the most rewarding aspects of this work.

## Illustrative Example of Plans for Dissemination and Utilization

**Effectiveness of Claim, Evidence, and Reasoning as an Innovation to Develop Students' Scientific Argumentative Writing Skills (Samosa, 2021)**

### Plan for Dissemination and Utilization

The research results will be cascaded to the School Principals, Head Teachers, Master Teachers, Curriculum Chairpersons and Classroom Teachers (Teacher I-III) in Graceville National High School the during school learning action cell sessions (SLACS); district, division and regional research conferences, and school governing council conference. These unspoiled avenues will be utilized to share reflections about current research results and recommend future actions beneficial to the K to 12 Science teachers- researcher. This present study also ensures that the research findings will be used for decision making on the utilization of the CER framework in the classroom context regardless of the field of specialization in support to the enhance basic education curriculum.

The findings of this study will also be utilized in the School Improvement Plan (SIP) of the Schools that encourage the teachers to be equip in creating innovation to improved students' academic performances. Nevertheless, other science teachers in the Division of City of San Jose del Bulacan, will be topped and encouraged to adopt the proposed innovation to developed students' scientific argumentative writing skills.

# CHAPTER 3

## GENERAL AND ACCCEPTABLE WRITING GUIDES FOR ACTION RESEARCH

**Learning Competency**
At the end of this module, teachers should be able to follow the general and acceptable writing guides for action research.

**General and Acceptable Writing Guides**

The action research follows the standard format for fonts, margins, spacing and the like, institutional formats and guidelines in writing other than DepEd Orders in the case of teachers in the basic education should also be considered.

**Fonts.** It is common observation that size 12 of Arial, Times New Romans, and Tahoma are the font types used in encoding action research. This varies depending on your institutions or divisions.

**Margins**. Ideally, facing the paper, 1.25" – right, 1.5" – left, 1" – top and bottom margins are generally observed. This has already the reserved space for cutting the edge and binding purposes. This may also be adjusted in the case that action research of the institution is required where there is an observed letterhead.

**Spacing**. Double space in all the discussions should be observed. Twenty to twenty-two (20-22) lines may be counted to make sure that the content in each page is double spaced. This may be lesser in the case of those institutions that require letterhead in all pages of the manuscript.

**Pagination.** There should be continuous pagination written in Arabic on top of the right-side margin from the 1st pages to the last page of the chapter. Page number is not reflected on first page of the chapter.

**Paper.** Usually, a paper with substance 20 (70 gsm), 8.5" x 11" is used as action research paper.

**Verb Tenses.** Use present form if it pertains to facts, while past action for opinion and claims. In general, verb tense should be in the following, although variations can occur within the text depending on the narrative style of your paper. Note that references to prior research mentioned anywhere in your paper should always be stated in the past tense.

1. Abstract – past tense (a summary description of what I did)
2. Introduction – present tense (I am describing the study to you now)
3. Literature Reviews – past tense (the studies you are reviewing have already been written)
4. Methodology – past tense (the way that you gathered and synthesized data already happened; otherwise, how could you write your paper)

5. Results – past tense (the findings have already been discovered)
6. Discussion – present tense (I am talking to you now about how I interpreted the findings)
7. Conclusion – present tense (I am summarizing the study for you now)

**Suggested Writing Guidelines (For a Research Proposal)**

**Introduction (Context and Rationale)**

1. Present a general description of the problem.
2. Show the relevance, timeliness and the need to address or improve the situation.
3. Discuss the nature and highlight of the identified problem or issue.
4. Elaborate different aspect of the action research setting showing the depth and critical analysis of the situation.
5. Include justification such as national, regional, division, district/school.

**Literature Review**

1. Cite theories and/or previous studies related to the present research.
2. Acknowledge the source properly.
3. Critically evaluate to identify inconsistencies or gaps in current knowledge or educational policy that the study intends to address.
4. Define and present constructs in a conceptual framework.
5. Citations must be consistent.

**Research Questions**

1. State aim, objective or general research question/s.
2. Specify the action research variables.
3. Key elements of the research questions should be reflected in the title.
4. Logically proceeds from the context.
5. Clearly relate to the identified problem and convey the desired change or improvement.

**Scope and Limitation**

1. Describe the coverage of the research in terms of location, time respondents etc.
2. Include parameters that can restrict the scope of the findings and are outside control of the researcher.

**Proposed Innovation, Intervention and Strategy**

1. Mention innovation, intervention or strategy to be done to address the problem.

2. Outline when and where the intervention, innovation will be done, and who will be involved.
3. State activities to be undertaken.
4. Explain in details the rationale extent and limitation of the intervention, innovation or strategy.

**Research Methodology**

- **Sampling**

Provide details about who will participate in the research and how will they be selected and recruited.

- **Respondents of the Study**

1. State the target participants and/or other sources of data and information such as learners, teachers, documents, realia, learner's product, etc.
2. Provide details of the target participants and/or other sources of data an information such as number, characteristics, sampling procedure if any.
3. Give clear rationale for their inclusion in the study.
4. Include voice of the people or customer in the discussion of the participants.

**Data Collection/Data Gathering Methods**

1. Present general descriptions of the method/s to be used in gathering the data.
2. Provide details of the gathering method/s such as specific kinds of data, how and when they will be collected (ex. Pretest and posttest scores).
3. Describe research instruments if any (ex. Text, scale, survey questionnaire, checklist, interview guide etc.)
4. Explain why the selected data gathering methods is appropriate to the nature and purpose of the action research.
5. Align method/s to the research questions.
6. Instruments should be appropriate for obtaining the desired data or information.

**Data Analysis Plan**

1. Present a general description on how the gathered data will be treated.
2. Give details of the method/s of data analysis.
3. Specify techniques (ex. Quantitative/statistical, qualitative, or both methods) as well as tools (ex. software) to be used.
4. Show appropriateness of the method used in data analysis to the nature of data gathered in addressing the research question/s.

**Ethical Considerations**

1. Identify ethical concerns that could emanate from the conduct of the research and discuss how to prevent these from taking place.

2. It may include but not limited to right to conduct a study or investigation to answer a question; secure free prior and informed consent from respondents, parents or guardians of learners, issues of confidentially and anonymity.

**Action / Work Plan**

1. List major activities and their timeliness.
2. Provide a detailed work plan covering start to the completion of the action research.
3. Timeliness are realistic and show concretely how the action research will unfold over the allowed period.
4. Reflect proponent's capacity to concretize ideas into clear and sequential steps to be done.

**Cost Estimates**

1. Include list of major items and their estimated costs as well as total cost.
2. Furnish a detailed breakdown of items with their corresponding costs.
3. Reflect the funding needs for the items and costs reasonably.
4. Reflect the proponent's capacity to project specific expenses that he/she will be accountable for.

**Plans for Dissemination, Utilization and Advocacy**

1. Indicate how the results will be cascaded to the intended user of the research findings (ex. Presentation in conferences etc.).

**References**

1. Use APA referencing.
2. Provide in – text of work and reference list consistently and accurate.

**Suggested Writing Guidelines (Additional for Full paper)**

**Title Page**

1. The title page announces the title of your action research, your name, the name and address of the school, and the date. Include also reference number if any.
2. Write the title in capital letters, one (1) inch from top single – spaced and in inverted pyramid. For other entries like "An Action Research presented to…" (refer to your institutional format and contents).
3. Name of the researcher is written in capital letters, complete with middle initial, two (2) inches from bottom of the page. In the case of more than

two researchers, enumerate names in alphabetical order or positions as researcher (such as chairman, member etc.).

4. Write the complete date, month and year, centered two (2) spaces below the name of the researcher.

**Abstract**

1. The abstract consists of 150 to 250 words as long as it fits the parameters in a single paragraph.
2. The abstract should be comprised of the following sentences:
    a) One to two sentence (s) covering the general context of the research topic.
    b) One to two sentence (s) regarding the specific research problems.
    c) One sentence regarding the research methodology.
    d) One to two sentences regarding the significant findings.
    e) Some institutions require a sentence regarding the conclusions and recommendations.
3. Remember there is no indention in this paragraph.
4. After the abstract, on the same page and starting a new paragraph are **keywords**, in italics, that will assist others in researching scholarly work related to your topic.

**Discussion of Results and Reflection**

1. This is otherwise the results and discussions as used in some institution. An introductory paragraph is provided at the start of the chapter.
2. The data may be presented in textual, graphical, and tabular ways.

**Principles of presentation of data in experimental, quantitative (survey) and qualitative studies**

**Experimental Studies**

Your data will be presented in the form of tables, graphs and diagrams, but you also need to use words to guide readers through your data:

1. Explain the tests your performed (and Why).
2. Explain how you gathered the data.
3. Present your results. Choose those that show something interesting and that your experiments support your conclusions. Show any negative results too, and try to explain them.
4. Indicate what results are significant.
5. Make meaningful comparisons.
6. Draw any immediate conclusions.

**Quantative (survey) studies**

These are generally accepted guidelines on how to display data and summarizes the results of statistical analyses of data about the population or group of people, plants or animals. However, this display needs to be presented in an informative way.

1. Describe the sample.
2. Remind the reader of the research question being addressed, or the hypothesis being tested.
3. Tell the reader what you want him/her to get from the data.
4. State which difference are significant.
5. Highlight the important trends and differences/comparisons.
6. Indicate whether the hypothesis is confirmed, not confirmed, or partially confirmed.

**Qualitative Studies**

The analysis of qualitative data cannot be neatly presented in tables and figures as quantitative results can be. It must all be expressed in words. This results in a large quantity of written material, through which you must guide your reader.

Structure is therefore very important. Try to make your sections and subsections reflect your thematic analysis of the data, and to make sure your reader knows how these themes evolve. Headings and subheadings, as well as directions to the reader, are forms of signposting you can use.

**Analysis** – Extracting ideas from the gathered data according to the questions stated in the statement of the problem.

**Interpretation** – What is in the table? For every table, there should be supporting literature and studies.

**Implication of the Findings** – consist of at least five elements:

1. The existence of a condition. This condition is a finding discovered in the research. The condition may be favorable or unfavorable. If it is favorable, it is strength of the subject studied. If it is unfavorable, it is a weakness of the subject.
2. The probable cause of the condition. If there is a condition there must be a logical relationship between the condition and the cause, otherwise the cause may not be a valid one.
3. The probable effect of the condition. Most likely, there is also a probable effect of the condition and there must be a logical relationship between the condition and its probable effect.
4. The measure to remedy the unsatisfactory condition or to continue to strengthen the favorable one. It is a natural to institute a measure to remedy an unfavorable one it is also a natural reaction to continue its operation and to even further strengthen it.

5. The entity or area involved or affected. The area directly affected by the unfavorable or favorable conditions discovered in the study should be cited more specifically.

**Recommendations**

1. Introduce first and present a detailed description of the suggestions for future action based on the significance of the conclusions. Include also recommendations for future research.

**Action Plan**

1. Indicate how the results of the action research will be utilized.
2. May be presented in a tabular form.

**Financial Report**

1. Present all financial aspect of your action research.
2. Include list of major items and their cost as well as total cost.
3. Furnish a detailed breakdown of items with their corresponding costs.
4. Reflect the funding needs for the items and costs reasonably.
5. Reflect the proponent's capacity to project specific expenses that he/she will be accountable for.

# BIBLIOGRAPHY


Almeida, A. B., et al. (2016). ***Research Fundamentals from Concept to Output: A Guide for Researcher and Thesis Writers.*** Adriana Printing Co.

Anol, B. (2012). ***Social Science Research: Principles, Methods and Practices***. Creative Commons Attribution-Noncommercial-Share Alike 3.0 Unpotted License.

Badke, W.B. (2012). ***Teaching Research Process: The Faculty's Role in the Development of Skilled Students Researchers***. CP Chados Publishing.

Bermudo, P. J., et al. (2010). ***Research Writing Made Simple: A Modular Approach for Collegiate and Graduate Students***. Mindshapes Corporation., Inc.

Calmorin, L. P., & Calmorin, M. A (2007). ***Research Methods and Thesis Writing 2nd Edition***. Rex Book Store.

Calmorin L. P. (2010a). ***Research and Statistics with Computer***. National Book Store.

Creswell, J. W. (2005). ***Educational research: Planning, conducting, and evaluating quantitative and qualitative research.*** Pearson Education, Inc.

Dela Cruz, N. V. (2011). ***A Guide to Thesis Writing.*** Research and Publication Office St. Dominic Savio College.

Flores, M. F. (2016). ***Methods of Research in Business Education.*** Unlimited Books Library Services & Publishing Inc.

Garcia, C. D. (2003). ***Fundamentals of Research and Research Designing***. Katha Publishing Co., Inc.

Gay, L. R. et al. (2012). ***Educational Research: Competencies for Analysis and Applications.*** Pearson Education, Inc.

Jesson, J. (2011). ***Doing Your Literature Review: Traditional and Systematic Techniques***. Sage.

Institute for Academic Development (2021). ***Literature review***. University of Edinburgh. https://www.ed.ac.uk/institute-academic-development/study-hub/learning-resources/literature-review.

Lapan, s., Quartaroli, M., & Riemer, F. (2012). ***An Introduction to Research Methods and Designs***. Jossey-Bass, A Wiley Imprint.

Mc Bride, D. M. (2013). ***Process of Research in Psychology***. Sage.

Morgan, D. L. (2014). ***Integrating Qualitative and Quantitative Methods: A Pragmatic Approach***. Sage.

Ochave, Jesus A. et al. (1992). ***Research Methods***. Rex Book Store.

Reyes, M. Z. (2004). ***Social Research: A Deductive Approach***. Rex Book Store.

Ridley, D. (2012). ***The Literature Review: A Step-by-Step Guide for Students.*** 2nd ed. Sage.

Samosa, R C. (2020). ***Understanding the End- to – End Praxis of Quantitative Research: From Scratch to Paper Presentation***. Book of Life Publication.

Samosa, R. C. (2020). ***The Praxis of Action Research in Mixed Method Design for Novice Teacher – Researchers***. Department of Education, Schools Division of City of San Jose del Monte Bulacan.

Samosa, R.C., Magulod, G.C., Capulso, L.B., Delos Reyes, R.J., Luna, AR. F., Maglente, S.S., Orte, CJ.S., Olitres, BJ.D., Pentang, J.P. Vidal, CJ. E. (2021). ***How to Write and Publish Your Thesis***. Beyond Books Publication.

Samosa, R. C. (2021***). Cultivating Research Culture: Capacity Building Program Toward Initiatives to Improve Teachers Self-Efficacy, Research Anxiety and Research Attitude***. European Scholar Journal, 2(3), 182-198. https://scholarzest.com/index.php/esj/article/view/385

Samosa, R.C. (2021). ***From Test Validity to Construct Validity & Back: Theory and Application in the Experimental Design in Science Action Research***. Philippine Association of Physics and Science Instructors,De La Salle University, Manila.

Samosa, R.C. (2021). ***Updates on Current Techniques in Action Research.*** Research Intellectual Discussion, Institute of Industry and Academic Research Incorporated.

Samosa, R. C. (2021). ***Effectiveness of Claim, Evidence and Reasoning as an Innovation to Develop Students' Scientific Argumentative Writing Skills***. Galaxy International Interdisciplinary Research Journal, 9(05), 135–150. https://doi.org/10.17605/OSF.IO/2PBW.

Resty C. Samosa. (2021). ***COSIM (COMICS CUM SIM): An Innovative Material in Teaching Biology.*** European Journal of Research Development and Sustainability, 2(4), 19-28. https://scholarzest.com/index.php/ejrds/article/view/44

Resty C. Samosa. (2021). ***Mobile Physics as Innovation to Reinvigorating Active Engagement and Learning Dynamics of Grade 11 Learners on Uniform Accelerated Motion***. International Journal for Research in Applied Sciences and Biotechnology, 8(2), 162-166. https://doi.org/10.31033/ijrasb.8.2.21

Samosa, R C. (2021). ***Cooperative Learning Approach as Innovation to Improve Students" Academic Achievement and Attitudes in Teaching***

***Biology.*** Journal of World Englishes and Educational Practices, 3(1). https://doi.org/10.32996/jweep.2021.3.1.1.

Samosa, R.C. (2021). ***Demystifying Research Gaps in Science, Technology, Engineering and Mathematics: Methods & Techniques***. 2nd Philippine Association of Physics and Science Instructors (PAPSI) International 3-Day Research Conference, De La Salle University, Manila.

Samosa, R. C., Amondina, K. N. C., Camposano, R. D., Ruadiel, A. P., Rayuan, C. J. P., & Soledad, N. J. Y. (2022). ***Virtual Laboratory as a Self-Paced Learning Innovation to Improve Learning Achievements and Attitudes in Teaching Physical Science***. British Journal of Innovation in Science, Research and Development, 1(2), 59-81.

Trinidad, J. E. (2018a). ***Researching Philippine Realities***. Ateneo De Manila University Press.

Trinidad, J. E. (2019b). ***Error – Proofing Your Research: Common Mistakes and How to Address Them***. Ateneo De Manila University Press.

Braun, V. & Clarke, V. (2006): Using thematic analysis in psychology, Qualitative Research in Psychology, 3:2, 77-101. http://dx.doi.org/10.1191/1478088706qp063oa.

Young, F. C. (2002). ***Fundamental of Research Writing Made Simple***. Bright Minds Publishing.

Zulueta, F. M., & Costales, NE B.(2003). ***Methods of Research, Thesis Writing and Applied Statistics***. National Book Store.

# ABOUT THE AUTHORS

## PROF. RESTY CALO. SAMOSA, PhDSciEd.

He is currently a full - time Senior High School Teacher, Research and Testing Coordinator of Graceville National High School and Professorial Lecturer in Colegio de San Gabriel Arcangel. He has taught courses in almost all facets of Natural Science and Research in Secondary and Tertiary Levels.

He obtained his license as educator in 2015. He continues to contribute to academe as researcher, innovator, resource speaker, lecturer, thesis adviser, statistician, evaluator, demonstration teacher, and paper presenter at various seminars, conferences, and science fairs.

Prof. Samosa fosters his professional growth by attending international, national, and regional conferences and seminar-workshop, and by being an active member of the Philippine Association for the Career Advancement of Educators (PACAE), Philippine Educational Measurement and Evaluation Association, Inc. (PAMEA) Biology Teachers Association of the Philippines (BIOTA),Philippine Association of Physics and Science Instructors (PAPSI) and Leadership in Education Academy & Development (LEAD) - Philippines.

He also published several textbooks includes the following Understanding the End- to End Praxis of Quantitative Research: From Proposal to Paper Presentation, General Biology 1, General Biology 2, General Chemistry 1, General Chemistry 2, Practical Research 2: Quantitative Research, Practical Research 1: Qualitative Research, Inquiries, Investigation, and Immersion, How to Write and Publish Your Thesis? : Practical Guide for Students & Teachers and How to Write and Publish Your Dissertation, Exploring the Essence & Meaning from the Sound of Experiences: Qualitative Research, Fundamentals of Earth Science, and From Proposal to Presentation: Demystifying Action Research Manual for Basic Education Teachers. In addition, he published research on high indexes international Journals; He also one of the Peer-Reviewers of the International Journal of Discoveries and Innovation in Applied Sciences, International Journal of Innovative Analyses and Emerging Technology, European Journal of Agricultural and Rural Education, International Review of Social Sciences Research and International Journal of Development and Public Policy.

He was the 2019 Action Research Champion in the 5th Division Research Congress for Teachers Category. He also won 2nd Outstanding Action Research

Paper in the 7$^{th}$ Division Research Congress for Teachers Category in the DepEd, City of San Jose del Monte, Bulacan. He also bagged the 2021 Global Outstanding Teacher (Leadership in Education Academy & Development-Philippines), 2021 Global Leader Award in Excellence Leadership & Global Educators Award in Research (Beyond Books Publication), 2021 Outstanding Teacher (World Educators Leaders' Summit & Awards), 2021 Outstanding Teacher in Research (Educacio World), 2021 Best Speaker in the Research Intellectual Discussions (Institute of Industry and Academic Research Incorporated in partnership with Universiti Teknologi Mara in Thailand), 2021 Outstanding Educator of Philippine Association of Physics Science Instructors (DLSU Manila) and 2020 Outstanding Teacher in Research (DepEd CSJM, Bulacan), 2022 Outstanding Learning Resource Developer (DepEd CSJM, Bulacan) and 2022 Outstanding Educator of Philippine Association of Physics Science Instructors (DLSU Manila).

## Rodrigo Mison Dantay, Jr. LPT, PhD-DEM, DPA, DLitt

Doc Rhodski is a graduate of Bachelor in Psychology major in Educational Psych at University of Caloocan City, he took his Master's in Education Major in Guidance and Counseling at EARIST Manila. He is a holder of three majorships in his Doctorate Degree - Doctor of Philosophy Major in Educational Management, Doctor of Public Administration and Doctor of Literature (Honorary Causa). He is a resource speaker of various institutions like United Coconut Planters Bank (UCPB), St. Benedict School, De La Salle, St. Anthony School, Arellano University, La Consolacion College, Our Lady of Guadalupe Seminary, Lyceum of the Philippines, Our Lady of Fatima University, and other private and public schools' INSET with topics relating to motivations, mental health, leadership, stress management, youth empowerment, team-capacity building, multiple intelligences, peace retreats and the likes.

He was the Philippine Representative to the ASEAN Youth Program held in Shizouka, Tokyo Japan. He is a licensed professional teacher. He was the Campus Administrator of University of Caloocan City Camarin Campus and BECED Department Head. Presently, he is the Department Chief of Housing and Resettlement Office of Caloocan City Hall and Regional Assessor of Department of Interior and Local Government (DILG). He is a panelist in Thesis and Dissertation Defenses as well as adviser to selected Graduate Students in their researches, He is a content and language editor of Rex Bookstore and Publishing Company, President of UCC Faculty Club Association, member of Pambansang Samahan ng Sikolohiyang Pilipino, Philippine Mental Health Association, Philippine Association for Graduate Education and International member of Gawad Ybarra Academia Española de Literatura. He is also an author of book about Guidance Services published internationally available at AMAZON.com and Padayon book available at Bookemon.com. He was awarded recently as an Outstanding Writer of the Philippines by Ophir Award giving body. He was also awarded as Best Filipino Public Servant - Leader by St. James University, USA. He is the Academic Consultant of Young Generation Academy and Lyceum ng Kabataan Academy. Speaker's Bureau Associate of Caloocan City Mayor Along Malapitan and Congressman Oscar Malapitan. He taught at Pamantasan ng Valenzuela and Colegio de Sta. Theresa. He is also a vlogger on his YouTube channel and FB Page of Doc Rhodski TV.

At top of these all, he loves teaching with subjects focusing on psychology, sociology and other social sciences to Bachelors, Masteral and Doctoral learners. He is happily married to Professor Rhea Cabueñas- Dantay who is also a licensed teacher and has a Masteral degree and pursuing Doctor in Educational Management. He loves to go out with his three vibrant children; Naomi, Alodia and Elijah during their free time.

www.ingramcontent.com/pod-product-compliance
Lightning Source LLC
LaVergne TN
LVHW080815170826
845678LV00011B/2010

* 9 7 8 6 2 1 4 7 0 3 9 8 2 *